KiDS CREATE

LAURIE CARLSON

KIDS CREATE

ART & CRAFT EXPERIENCES FOR KIDS

GIBBS SMITH
TO ENRICH AND INSPIRE HUMANKIND

CONTENTS

KIDS CREATE!

Kids Create! is a collection of art and craft projects for children ages 4 through 9 years. The younger children will need quite a bit of guidance in using the materials, but they will benefit from the fun of using different mediums, as well as the practice in refining their motor skills. Children in the midrange may be able to read the instructions themselves and will very likely be able to follow the illustrations. These children, too, will benefit from the help and input of an adult. Older children may well be able to use this book on their own, perhaps asking for some guidance in assembling materials and in using hot glue, craft knives, and paraffin.

Most of the materials are readily available in many homes. Feel free to substitute wherever needed as these items are merely suggestions. As much as possible, I have tried to avoid using materials which are harmful to the environment. No project uses specially purchased Styrofoam items. In some cases, I

mention items such as trays used to package meats. Obviously, we need to work toward ridding our environment of these harmful packaging materials, but since they are presently still widely available, rather than throw them away, save them to recycle in various art and craft projects. In fact, it is a good idea to collect these trays as well as egg cartons to give to school craft programs. At the very least, this will keep these items out of our landfills. Plastic wrap has been omitted from every project. There are many suitable substitutes. Art and craft projects should be environmentally friendly; part of the creativity for children should involve finding and using biodegradable materials whose production and disposal are environmentally sound.

WHY KIDS LOVE ARTS & CRAFTS

The joy of creating something is exhilarating. Children, especially, enjoy the creative process, loving every minute of the making. Creative thinking and personal emotion combine into an individual's artistic expression—a kind of expression where there is no right or wrong.

Making art fulfills children's real need for self-expression. They

are eager to experience life and to participate actively and imaginatively in it.

Children crave the creative outlet that making things provides. We cheat them if we only offer them a life of television and other passive activities. Children who are deprived of opportunities for self-expression through the arts often seek other emotional and creative outlets. Behavior, dress, and interests reflect this unmet need. Street graffiti, unusual hairstyles, and strong identification with peer groups become the only available forms of self-expression.

The zest for art is easy to recognize in young children. It doesn't disappear as they get older, as some would have you think. It isn't a phase that children outgrow. The desire to express oneself is ongoing, still present at all ages. Unfortunately, as we get older, we become more inhibited. We begin to judge our efforts as compared to some idea of perfection that we hold. We forget that we can create just for the fun of it.

Children ages 3 to 9 still feel very free to express themselves artistically. Any form of hesitation or withdrawal usually has more to do with factors other than the task at hand. If we, as adults, continually provide these younger children with opportunities to refine their motor skills, to become familiar with various media, to feel proud of each and every creation, we give our children multiple gifts. They are more likely to approach the preteen and teen years with greater confidence and a valuable awareness that artistic expression is a pleasurable, available, acceptable, creative, and emotional outlet.

As you discover, along with your children, the freedom and adventure that art can provide, leave inhibitions behind and have fun! The value of the activity isn't measured in the finished product, but rather in the pure enjoyment and learning along the way.

USING THIS BOOK

Some of us adults have allowed our creative impulses to become stifled. We feel we lack the imagination and freedom to lead our children in creating art. For us, I've included some structured projects in this book. Use them as a springboard for your own ideas and variations. Use the suggested project design as a starting point, not as a rigid parameter to be strictly copied. When a pattern is shown, it's to give you a suggested size or shape. If you want to try a project in the book but lack something on the materials list, don't hesitate to

look for something that could be substituted. Except for the clay dough recipes, there really are no absolutes; using different materials can result in a wider variety of experiences.

Use the ideas in this book as a starting point for your own creative expression, as well as the children's. Experiment, change, and push the limits of each project or media you try. As adults we tend to let our lack of creative confidence limit what we try. Urge yourself to try new materials and different ways of using them. By conveying an attitude of capable confidence toward making art, your children will sense that they, too, are free to explore and create. Refrain from criticizing your own efforts or your child's. If something turns out differently than you had planned, greet it as a great innovation, not a grave disappointment. Avoid even thinking in terms of failure, or a right or wrong way, or even a better way. Children pick up these unspoken messages, leading them to criticize their work and doubt their ability.

Remember, there are no rights or wrongs (no failures) in crafting. Every time a child tries something, he or she is enlarging a skills repertoire and increasing the scope of creative thinking. For all of us the possibilities are always

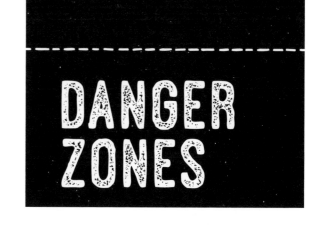

DANGER ZONES

To ensure the safety and well-being of your young artists and artisans, please observe these safety measures.

Paraffin: Wax and paraffin should be melted in a can placed in the top of a double boiler (water in both parts of double boiler). An adult must always do this part of a project. Paraffin is flammable.

Hot glue gun: This is very handy, but must be used by adults only.

Balloons: Balloons may seem innocent and fun, but they can be deadly to toddlers who swallow deflated balloons or balloon pieces. Please use with care around young children.

Craft knives: Adults should use the craft knives and sharp scissors, demonstrating correct methods for safe use and handling.

Ventilation: Proper ventilation is necessary when using rubber cement and many fixatives. Acrylic sprays are extremely flammable as well as toxic. (Hair spray is a good substitute.) Adults should spray fixatives, not children.

endless. So, enjoy, encourage, and excite yourself and your child with art. The world gives us all so many restrictions, criticisms, and putdowns. Let creating together be a door you help your child open—a door to personal satisfaction, pride, and enjoyment. Along the way you and your child can enjoy some truly quality time together: exploring ideas, creating from within, laughing together, and patting one another on the back.

Let the joy and excitement of creating something of their own give your children the confidence and courage to hold on to the creative innocence of childhood for a lifetime.

Use the ideas in this book to unlock your own creative processes. As you become more confident about providing creative opportunities for your child, you will be able to adapt and expand these beginnings into a multitude of ideas involving a variety of media.

Now, find those scissors, mix the paint, turn on your imagination, and let's begin!

KEYS TO CONFIDENCE

Each project is identified as to the approximate degree of difficulty involved in confidently completing it. Look for the paintbrushes to identify the suggested range of ability or dexterity each project might involve.

1 Brush= Few fine motor skills needed. Adults may need to help very young children by preparing some of the materials ahead of time. These projects should delight most children with very little adult assistance.

2 Brushes= Skills such as cutting, folding, using a template, or painting may be required. Young children need practice with these skills, but adults should avoid creating frustrating experiences for those truly too young to handle them. Most children enjoy these projects, and will experiment with the wider range of mediums and tools.

3 Brushes= More involved projects that require manual dexterity and a variety of steps to complete.

CLOCK WATCHERS

Because time allowances are necessary for using some mediums and completing some of the projects, I've identified projects that require more than one hour to complete. Look for the little clock, which is your signal that this project takes more than one hour. Read through these projects, because many of them have convenient stopping points.

If you can leave your materials out and come back later, the time may not be a factor.

In some cases, materials must be prepared ahead of time, or a drying or baking time is required. This is not included in the hour estimate. Allow extra time for drying, which varies with the medium used, the thickness of the project, humidity levels, and temperatures.

These keys are quite arbitrary. Don't let them limit your choice of project. If a project is interesting, fun, and appropriate in nature, work around any part that seems beyond the children. Kids are extremely versatile, especially when they really want to do something. Usually they are very willing to stretch their abilities or find clever shortcuts.

PAPER AND PASTE

THE FIRST CRAFT MATERIAL MOST CHILDREN ARE INTRODUCED TO IS PAPER.

It's easy for even the youngest child to manipulate paper by folding, cutting, and scribbling. When paste is added, the possibilities are endless. The types and varieties of paper available provide many different ways to do a project. Keep a box for storing the unusual papers you find: gift wrap, tissue, cellophane, lightweight cardboard, textured grass cloth, embossed wallpapers, crepe paper, wax paper, even computer printout paper (useful for painting banners or drawing murals). Keep this assortment of papers handy, letting children experiment with folding, cutting, and pasting the different types.

PASTES & GLUES

Pastes and glues vary in their kinds and uses, too. The school pastes are not used as much as in the past, because they are thick, hard to spread, and crumble when dry. They are, however, inexpensive and don't spill. White glue is a favorite with children. It is washable and can be diluted with water to make spreading easier for young fingers. It dries clear. Glue sticks are handy for small projects that need a small amount of adhesive. Rubber cement is useful for mounting papers on mat board for display. It dries smooth, leaving no bumps beneath the paper. It doesn't apply easily, though, because it dries so quickly. An uncovered container will dry out very quickly. Rubber cement is more practical for an older child's use. Hot glue guns are useful for many craft projects. They definitely require an adult's supervision because they can be dangerous. The gun and glue reach high temperatures that can easily burn young hands.

SCISSORS & OTHER TOOLS

There are some other tools that make creating with paper easier and widen the possibilities. You'll want to have several types of scissors: safety scissors for the young children and pointed scissors for the older ones who need to snip in tiny areas. Pinking shears are fun to use, too. For cutting heavy cardboard and other craft materials, a craft knife is desirable. Craft knives come in a variety of designs. They are all sharp and should only be used by an adult who is assisting the child. Even older children need adult direction and supervision when using them. Other tools you'll find useful are hole punches, staplers, rulers, metal brads, and paper clips.

Preschool children need lots of practice honing their fine motor skills. Safety scissors and scraps of paper will keep them busy. Encourage these children to cut in different ways, creating shapes and patterns with the paper. Show them how to draw a line, and then cut along it. This gives them practice at eye-hand coordination, an important skill needed for later school success.

Simply cutting papers into geometric shapes can be fun and challenging for older children as well. Find examples of fine paper-cutting, called scherenschnitte, in a library book and encourage them to try the delicate craft using nail scissors and rice paper.

Paper can also be cut into strips, rolled in coils, then glued down to create designs. Called quilling, it is a project that can vary in difficulty depending on the age and ability of the artist.

Just playing with papers, pastes, and a few tools should get creative juices flowing. Read on for a few ideas you might not have thought of, then get out the box of supplies and see what you can come up with. Remember, most papers are inexpensive, so feel free to experiment and let your child try things you and I might not have considered.

QUILL PEN

What's the first thing you need in order to send a special letter? It's a pen, of course! Here's how to make a real quill pen to sign your John Hancock—otherwise known as your name.

With a knife or scissors, cut a slant at the tip of the feather's quill. This slant allows the ink to flow down from the quill to the paper when you press the feather to paper.

To load the pen, dip the cut part of the feather into ink or tempera paint thinned with a little water. Practice writing on scrap paper first. Keep a paper towel handy to blot excess ink. If your quill pen tip gets worn down, cut a bit more off, at a slant, and it will be new again.

MATERIALS

SHARP KNIFE OR SCISSORS

BIRD FEATHER
(CHICKEN OR TURKEY ARE BEST)

INK OR THINNED TEMPERA PAINT

CUT THE
FEATHER AT
A SLANT

SEND A LETTER

FOLD THE LETTER TWICE

PLACE THE LETTER OR CARD IN THE
CENTER OF ENVELOPE PAPER

FOLD SIDE
IN & GLUE

FOLD IN
THIRDS

GLUE FLAP
DOWN

ENVELOPES ARE EASY

Envelopes can be made from almost any type of paper: gift wrap, shopping bags, aluminum foil, colored papers, wallpaper sample pages, or printer paper.

Before making an envelope, write the letter or create the card you want to put in it. Then make the envelope to fit the size you need.

To create an envelope, lay out a piece of paper the size of your letter. Fold the letter once each way and lay it in the center of the envelope paper. Fold the two sides around the letter and glue. Fold in thirds from top to bottom. Fold up from the bottom. Use some glue to dot the edges of the top flap and fold it over. Press.

To create an envelope for a card, use paper four times the size of the card, and lay the card the same as you did the letter.

MATERIALS

PAPER

WHITE GLUE, GLUE STICK, OR PASTE

11

POP-UP CARD

One type of pop-up card is made from a piece of 8 x 10-inch paper. Fold it in half lengthwise. Cut out a 3 x 3-inch notch. Fold the remaining portion that juts out down inside the card at an angle. This will be the piece that pops up when the card is opened. Cut into any shape, such as a heart, or cut into an oval with a face drawn on it. Decorate the front cover of the card as you wish and add your message.

Another pop-up card is made with construction paper and paste or glue. Make a greeting card. Decide what design you want to pop up from your card. Some ideas are balloon shapes, a birthday cake, a sun, a heart, Christmas designs, or a message bubble. Draw and color the pop-up piece on a separate piece of paper. Cut it out. Cut a small strip of paper about 1/2 inch wide and 3 inches long. Fold accordion-style in small folds. Glue one end to position inside the card. Trim the strip so it pops up about 1 inch. Glue your cut-out design to the other end of the strip.

MATERIALS

PAPER

SCISSORS

CRAYONS, MARKERS, OR PAINTS

GLUE

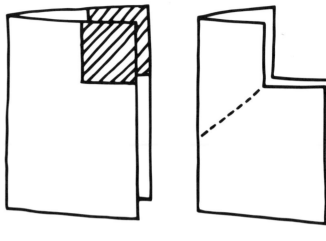

CUT AWAY THE 3 X 3-INCH PORTIONS

FOLD THE TOP PART TO THE INSIDE, ON AN ANGLE

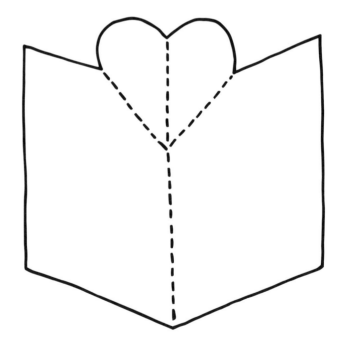

IT WILL POP UP WHEN OPENED

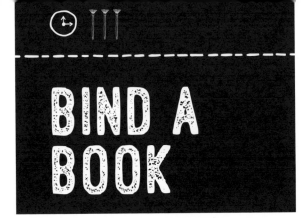

BIND A BOOK

Lay the piece of fabric on a table with the wrong side facing up. Position the cardboard pieces as shown. The small piece of cardboard will be the book's spine. Leave a 1/8-inch space between the spine and the other pieces of cardboard to make it easy to turn the pages.

Spread glue on the back of the cardboard and reposition on the fabric. Press into place firmly. Let dry.

Turn the edges of fabric up over the cardboard. Fold the corners in to miter them (neatly at an angle). Glue down. Let dry.

Using 5 pieces of printer paper at a time, fold the papers in half. Stitch them together with the needle and thread down the creased middle. You will have 5 of these little booklets.

Stack them together with the stitched spines touching. Apply glue to the spines and cover with a heavy weight, such as a telephone book. Dry.

Place the book pages on the cover spine.

For the inside cover or flyleaf, decorate some printer paper or use something special, such as gift wrap. This will be the decorative inside cover of your book. Cut two flyleaf papers to 8 x 1 inches each. Place one flyleaf sheet over the inside front cover, and glue to the first page of the book. Repeat at the last page and back inside cover. This will hold the book together.

Now, start writing!

1/8-INCH SPACE   SPINE

TUCK THE CORNERS IN AND GLUE IN PLACE

MATERIALS

FABRIC:
1 (11 X 15 1/2-INCH) PIECE

CARDBOARD:
2 (6 1/4 X 9 1/4-INCH) PIECES AND 1 (1/2 X 9 1/4-INCH) PIECE

RULER

WHITE GLUE

PRINTER PAPER: 25 SHEETS

SCISSORS

NEEDLE & THREAD

SPECIAL GIFT WRAP PAPER FOR THE INSIDE COVER (OPTIONAL)

IT'S EASY TO MAKE A BOUND BOOK FOR WRITING POETRY, STORIES, OR TO USE AS A JOURNAL TO RECORD YOUR THOUGHTS ON LIFE.

JIGSAW PUZZLE

Trim the cardboard so it is the same size as the picture. Spread the back of the picture with rubber cement and glue to the cardboard. Dry. Turn the cardboard over and use pencil to draw curving lines from one edge of the cardboard to the other. Draw more curving shapes within the larger ones. Don't make the areas too small, or cutting them out will be difficult. When you have divided the area into interesting shapes, cut along the lines to create the puzzle pieces.

Store pieces in an envelope. If you want to make the puzzle more durable, cover the picture with a piece of clear adhesive paper before cutting.

If you make several puzzles, you may want to label them so they don't get mixed up. Label the pieces that go with each puzzle by marking them with a similar mark, such as a colored "x" on the back of one puzzle's pieces, and an "s" on all pieces to another puzzle.

GLUE PICTURE
TO THE CARDBOARD

MATERIALS

SCISSORS

LIGHTWEIGHT CARDBOARD
(NOTEBOOK COVER, TAGBOARD, SHIRT CARDBOARD)

POSTER OR MAGAZINE PICTURE

PENCIL

RUBBER CEMENT

CLEAR ADHESIVE PAPER
IF DESIRED (LIKE CONTACT BRAND)

DRAW A PUZZLE PATTERN
ON THE CARDBOARD.
CUT THE PUZZLE APART
ON THE LINES

DOORKNOB HANGERS

Draw and cut out several basic hanger shapes using the pattern shown. Use the markers to decorate, draw, and write messages on the hangers. Some ideas you might want to use are:

DO NOT DISTURB

NO ADULTS ALLOWED

ON VACATION

MAID SERVICE

GREAT BRAIN AT WORK

HOME OF THE MAIN BRAIN

QUIET: KID AT WORK

MATERIALS

SCISSORS

LIGHTWEIGHT CARDBOARD OR TAGBOARD

COLORED MARKERS

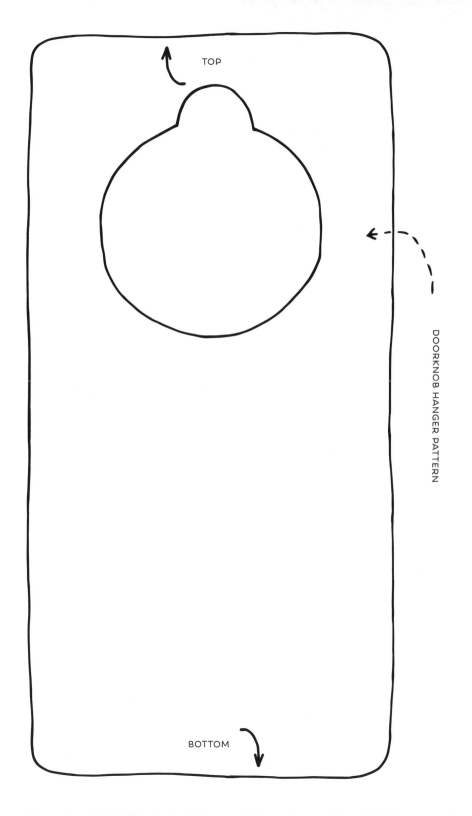

TOP

DOORKNOB HANGER PATTERN

BOTTOM

15

HOMEMADE PAPER

Fill the blender 2/3 full of warm water. While blending at low speed, drop strips of newspaper in, one at a time, through the lid. Blend until thick and pulpy. Place the screens over the cut openings of the dishpans. Set the dishpans inside each other and over the third, larger dishpan (or sink) to drain.

Slowly pour the pulp onto the screens. Allow water to drain off. Remove the screens. The pulp will stick to the top one. Place the pulp mass, screen side down, on a towel. Cover the pulp with the other screen. Roll gently but firmly with a rolling pin to squeeze out more water. Now gently peel the pulp from the screen. Lay it on a flat towel. Cover with the piece of sheet and iron to remove more moisture. Let paper dry overnight.

If you want to add some color to your paper, use torn colored shopping bags instead of newspapers. You can also add objects, such as feathers, flower petals, or confetti, to give different textures and interesting effects. If you place a flat object under the pulp mass before it is ironed, you can emboss a design on the finished paper. Use coins, leaves, or tagboard cutouts for embossing.

You can make your own paper in the kitchen or outdoors. Use a location where an electrical outlet is handy for the blender and a little messiness won't be a problem.

Once your paper is dry, you can write on it with markers or watercolors. Haiku poetry done with pen and ink looks very nice on homemade paper. Calligraphy is fun, too.

(Special markers are available for calligraphic writing.)

MATERIALS

BLENDER

WARM WATER (ROOM TEMPERATURE WILL WORK)

NEWSPAPERS, TORN IN 1 X 2–INCH STRIPS*

2 PIECES OF WIRE WINDOW SCREEN, CUT TO FIT THE BOTTOM OF THE DISHPANS

2 PLASTIC DISHPANS (SAME SIZE), BOTTOMS CUT OUT WITH A CRAFT KNIFE

1 LARGER DISHPAN (OR SINK), FOR DRAINING THE EXCESS WATER

2 TO 3 TOWELS

ROLLING PIN

BEDSHEET: 1 (12 X 12–INCH) PIECE

STEAM IRON

TWO SMALLER PANS HAVE BOTTOMS CUT OUT

TWO PIECES OF SCREEN

POSITION OF PANS WHEN DRAINING

*ONE–HALF OF A FULL–SIZE DOUBLE SHEET OF NEWSPAPER SEEMS TO BE ALL A BLENDER CAN HANDLE AT ONE TIME. IT YIELDS PAPER APPROXIMATELY 8 X 8 INCHES. DON'T USE THE ADVERTISING SECTIONS THAT ARE PRINTED ON SLICK COLORED PAPER, AS THE FINISH WON'T ALLOW THE PAPER TO ABSORB WATER.

PERISCOPE

Using the mirrors as patterns, trace around them near the bottom of two sides of the box on opposite ends, as shown in diagram. Cut the two sections out. Place the mirrors at an angle inside the box, opposite the cut out openings. Use tape to hold them in place. Adjust the mirrors until you can see out of the top hole by looking into the bottom hole. Use the hot glue gun to glue the mirrors in place along their edges.

Put the lid back on the box. Seal the lid to the box with masking tape.

MATERIALS

2 SMALL MIRRORS

NARROW BOX, LIKE A SHOE BOX, WITH A LID

SCISSORS

MASKING TAPE

HOT GLUE GUN

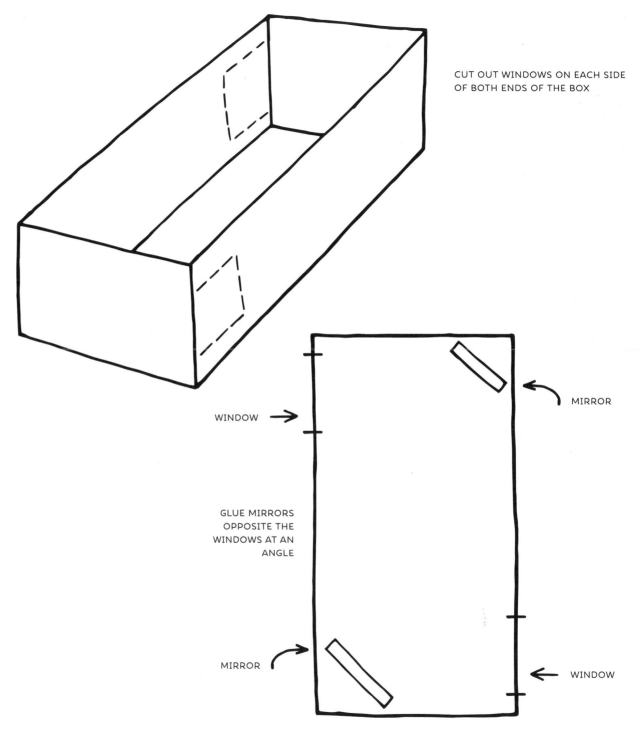

CUT OUT WINDOWS ON EACH SIDE OF BOTH ENDS OF THE BOX

WINDOW →

← MIRROR

GLUE MIRRORS OPPOSITE THE WINDOWS AT AN ANGLE

MIRROR →

← WINDOW

ZANY BALLOON PEOPLE

Blow up the balloon and knot the end.

Draw the pattern shown to create feet with shoes. If you want bare feet, draw on toes. Trace the pattern with tissue paper, then use that to draw the foot shape onto the tagboard. Cut the foot section from the poster board. Cut slits as shown. Decorate the feet with markers as you desire. Shoe laces can be inserted into the tagboard by threading yarn through holes made with a paper punch. Insert the knotted end of the balloon into the feet, so the balloon person will stand up.

Now decorate the balloon with markers to create facial features, hair, eyeglasses, or whatever. Cut out ears, jewelry, or head bands from construction paper and glue in place. Hair can be made by gluing sections of yarn on

the balloon or by cutting long narrow strips of tissue paper, curling them around a pencil, and then gluing curls in place.

See warning, page 69.

MATERIALS

BALLOON*

TISSUE PAPER

POSTERBOARD:
1 (12 X 12-INCH) PIECE

SCISSORS

FELT-TIP MARKERS,
(WASHABLE-TYPE
PERMANENT INKS TEND TO
BREAK THE BALLOON)

CONSTRUCTION PAPER

YARN

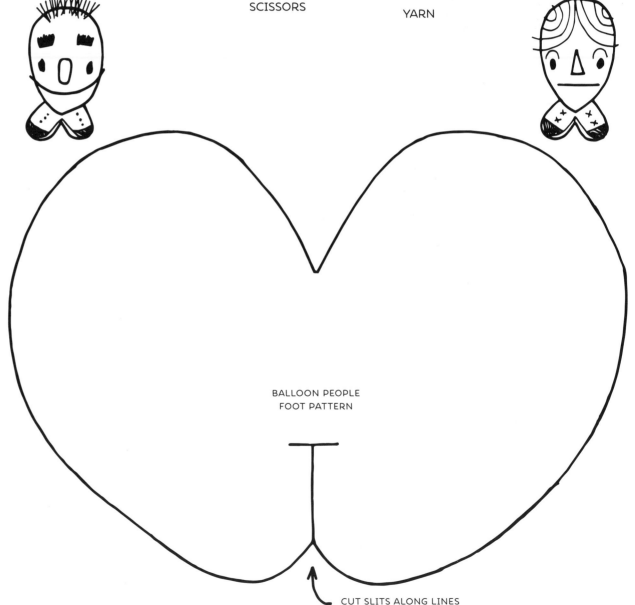

BALLOON PEOPLE
FOOT PATTERN

CUT SLITS ALONG LINES

BIG MOUTH PUPPETS

Tape the open end of the gelatin box closed. Use scissors to cut across the middle and two sides of the box. Don't cut the other broad side. Fold the box in half along the uncut side. This box will be the puppet's mouth.

Cut across the toe of the sock, about 2 inches from the end. Slip the sock over the box so it creates a head and neck for the puppet. You may have to cut a larger opening in the sock to get it to fit over the box. Glue the sock to the box. Use the fabric scraps to cover the box, and then decorate both the box and sock, creating a character of your choice. Felt teeth can be glued inside the open mouth, and a red oval glued in place can be a tongue. Glue on the plastic eyes or make your own from felt scraps.

Bring the puppet to life by placing your arm inside the sock and your fingers in the box halves.

MATERIALS

1 EMPTY GELATIN BOX FOR EACH PUPPET

SCISSORS

1 SOCK

GLUE & TAPE

FABRIC SCRAPS, POMPOMS, YARN, SEQUINS, FELT

GLUE-ON EYES: HOMEMADE OR STOREBOUGHT

CUT 2 INCHES OFF THE TOE OF THE SOCK

CUT BOX OPEN ON 3 SIDES

FOLD BOX HALVES IN THE MIDDLE

GLUE END OF SOCK OVER BOX AND DECORATE

"ME" PUPPET

Take a good look at yourself. Look at your hairstyle, hair color, and clothing. Then draw yourself on the tagboard and color in all details. Draw big, using the whole piece of paper. Make sure the arms and legs and neck are strong and thick.

Cut out. Trace your cut out figure on another piece of tagboard for the back of the puppet. Cut out. Color it like a back view of yourself. Staple or glue all around the edges, leaving the bottom open.

Make a newspaper stick by folding the paper in 1-inch folds, starting at a corner. Fold the paper and tape at the middle. Cut off the ends to even them up. Insert the end of the newspaper roll into the puppet and staple or tape to secure.

For fun, make a whole family of puppets, including your dog and cat!

MATERIALS

CONSTRUCTION PAPER OR TAGBOARD: 2 (9 X 12-INCH) PIECES

CRAYONS

PENCIL

SCISSORS

STAPLER OR GLUE

TAPE

NEWSPAPER

MAKE A STICK FROM ROLLED AND TAPED NEWSPAPER

STAPLE FRONT TO BACK WITH STICK IN BETWEEN

SILHOUETTES

Silhouettes are an old-fashioned form of portraiture. Work with a friend to create silhouettes. Set up a projector with no film in it. (You can shine a strong flashlight through a tissue paper roll.) Project the light onto a plain wall. Sit in front of the projector light so that the light shines on the side of your face. Your profile will project onto the wall behind you. Have your helper tape the piece of black construction paper to the wall. Then, using white chalk or white crayon, your helper should trace the outline of your profile onto the black paper.

When the tracing is finished, carefully cut your profile out and glue it to the piece of white paper.

Use the same method to create silhouettes of toys, plants, or an abstract that might create an interesting outline. Just set the objects on a table in front of the projector.

Some silhouettes can be made without using a bright light or projector. Draw action figures, scenes showing people and animals running, jumping, boxing, falling, or whatever. Don't worry about any details, just show the outlines of the figures. Draw on white paper and cut out along the outlines. Then trace onto black paper. Cut out carefully and glue to a larger piece of white paper.

MATERIALS

PROJECTOR

CONSTRUCTION PAPER:
1 BLACK AND 1 WHITE PIECE,
EACH 12 X 18 INCHES

CHALK OR WHITE CRAYON

SCISSORS

PHOTO STATUES

MAKE A FAVORITE PHOTOGRAPH EXTRA SPECIAL BY TURNING IT INTO A FREE-STANDING SCULPTURE.

Use scissors to carefully cut around the outline or outside edges of the photo's subject. Spray the back of the photo with the spray adhesive and glue it to the foam core board. When the adhesive is dry, cut the foam board to fit the photo with a sharp craft knife. Cut by gently slicing around the outline until it is cut evenly. Leave a straight edge at the bottom of the photo. Paint or stain the wooden strips as desired. Glue the photo between the two strips of wood. They will form a base, enabling the photo sculpture to stand alone.

MATERIALS

SCISSORS

PHOTOGRAPH, ENLARGED TO 8 X 10 INCHES, IF POSSIBLE

SPRAY ADHESIVE

FOAM CORE BOARD (A LIGHTWEIGHT FOAM BOARD AVAILABLE IN ART SUPPLY STORES)

CRAFT KNIFE

PAINT OR STAIN

TWO STRIPS OF WOOD MOLDING (AS LONG AS THE PICTURE'S BASE)

WHITE GLUE

GLUE PHOTO TO FOAM CORE.

GLUE WOOD STRIPS TO FRONT AND BACK OF FOAM

CUT-PAPER MOSAICS

Cut small pieces of construction paper, sorting them by colors into small containers or boxes. You can use a pencil to outline your design on the construction paper background or begin by gluing tesserae onto the background. Fill in all areas with cut paper pieces, allowing some background to show if you wish.

MATERIALS

SCISSORS

COLORED CONSTRUCTION PAPER

SMALL BOXES TO SORT THE TESSERAE

GLUE: DILUTE WHITE GLUE WITH A LITTLE WATER OR USE PASTE OR RUBBER CEMENT

CONSTRUCTION PAPER, ILLUSTRATION BOARD, TAG BOARD, OR GIFT BOXES TO GLUE THE TESSERAE ONTO

THIS PROJECT IS GOOD TO USE UP ALL YOUR SCRAPS OF COLORED PAPER. TESSERAE (A BIG WORD FOR SMALL PIECES OF PAPER) ARE USED. THEY ARE STRIPS OF COLORED CONSTRUCTION PAPER CUT INTO 1/2-INCH OR 3/4-INCH PIECES.

CUT-PAPER ART

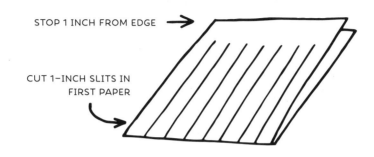

STOP 1 INCH FROM EDGE

CUT 1-INCH SLITS IN FIRST PAPER

TRIM 1-INCH STRIPS FROM SECOND PAPER

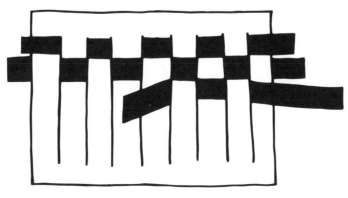

WEAVE STRIPS OVER AND UNDER SLITS

WEAVE A PICTURE

Find two brightly colored pictures and trim them so they are the same size. Fold one picture in half horizontally. Starting at the fold, draw vertical lines about one inch apart, ending about an inch from the edge of the paper. Cut along the lines and open the picture flat.

On the second picture, draw horizontal lines about one inch apart. Cut one strip at a time from the second picture. Weave each strip into the first picture, which now serves as a paper "loom." Cut and weave one strip at a time, going over—then under—each paper strip. Make sure each strip is facing the same direction. Tape the edges in place as you go. When finished, you will have two pictures blended together, creating an interesting composition. Glue the woven picture onto a larger piece of colored construction paper, if you wish.

MATERIALS

PICTURES CUT FROM MAGAZINES

SCISSORS & TAPE

GOLD MEDALS

Trace a circle onto the construction paper using the jar lid as a template. Cut out. Moisten the back of the notary seal and stick it onto the circle, or glue a foil seal on. Punch a hole in the top of the paper circle and thread the length of ribbon through it. Knot the ends. With a marker, write whatever inscription you'd like (Best Sport) onto the gold emblem.

MATERIALS

CONSTRUCTION PAPER: RED, WHITE, OR BLUE

JAR LID TO TRACE A CIRCLE

NOTARY SEAL (GOLD FOIL STAR EMBLEMS FOUND IN STATIONERY STORES OR MADE FROM ALUMINUM FOIL)

1 (30-INCH) LENGTH OF RIBBON: RED, WHITE, OR BLUE

HOLE PUNCH

FINE-TIP PERMANENT MARKER

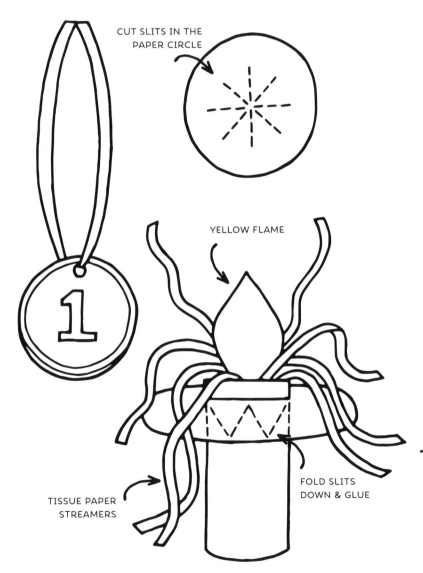

CUT SLITS IN THE PAPER CIRCLE

YELLOW FLAME

TISSUE PAPER STREAMERS

FOLD SLITS DOWN & GLUE

PAPER TORCHES

Cut a flame shape from the yellow paper. Cut and glue the white paper to cover the tube. Cut a large circle from the white paper (use a coffee can lid for a pattern). Cut two "x" shapes in the center to create slits. Push the paper circle down about one inch from the end of the tube, folding back the slits. Glue into place. Glue the yellow flame shape to the top end of the tube.

Cut strips of the colored tissue paper, about 12 inches long and 1/4 inch wide. Glue them to the tube next to the flame shape.

Take off running with your torch, and the colored tissue will wave from the torch and appear to be flames. A large torch can be created using tubes from gift wrap, a paper plate for the circle shape, and longer pieces of tissue paper.

MATERIALS

SCISSORS

CONSTRUCTION PAPER: WHITE AND YELLOW

PAPER TOWEL OR TOILET PAPER TUBES

COFFEE CAN LID FOR TEMPLATE

GLUE

TISSUE PAPER: RED, ORANGE, YELLOW

PIONEER LOG CABIN

Cut the paper bags into 4-inch-wide strips. Cut the strips into 2 1/2-inch-long pieces. To make a log, roll the strip around the pencil and glue the cut end. Slide the cylinder off the pencil and repeat. When you have about 16 of these cylinders (logs) made, you are ready to construct the base of the cabin.

Arrange the logs on a paper plate, alternating the logs at the corners. Glue them together. Glue a second row of logs on top of the first, staggering them at the corners. Continue building upward until your cabin is four logs high.

Roll some smaller logs. Use 2 (3 x 2 1/2-inch) strips to make logs for the first row that will taper to the roof. Then make three more pairs of logs, with each pair getting a little shorter than the last. Glue them at opposite ends of the cabin. Glue longer ones on first and taper to the roofline.

Fold the brown construction paper in half and adjust the size to fit your cabin. Glue it atop the logs.

You can use small pieces of the grocery bags or colored paper to create a chimney, windows, shutters, a porch step, or whatever details you choose.

MATERIALS

SCISSORS	WHITE GLUE
BROWN PAPER GROCERY BAGS	PAPER PLATE
PENCIL	BROWN CONSTRUCTION PAPER: 1 (8 X 8-INCH) PIECE

GLUE LOGS INTO PLACE

CUT PAPER DOORS AND WINDOWS

ROLL PAPER AND GLUE

WIGWAMS

Paint or color the outside of the filter. Cut a hole for a doorway. Wigwams were made from branches and grasses held together with mud. To make yours look more realistic, glue on bits of straw or cut paper.

MATERIALS

BROWN TEMPERA PAINT OR MARKER

PAPER COFFEE FILTERS (THE FLAT-BOTTOMED KIND)

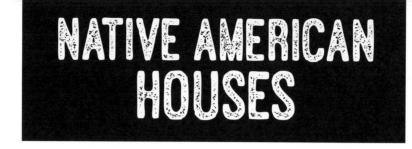

NATIVE AMERICAN HOUSES

NATIVE AMERICAN INDIANS LIVED IN DIFFERENT KINDS OF HOUSES, DEPENDING UPON WHICH TRIBE THEY BELONGED TO AND WHERE THEY LIVED. HERE ARE TWO TYPES.

TEPEES

Cut the paper plate in half. One half will make one tepee. Decorate the plate with Native American designs using colorful markers or paints. Roll the cut ends together to create a cone and staple. Trim a bit of the point away to insert drinking straws so they stick out of the top to look like the lodge poles the Native Americans used to keep their houses upright. Cut a slit from the bottom and fold the edges back toward the tepee to create a door.

MATERIALS

SCISSORS

PAPER PLATE

MARKING PENS OR TEMPERA PAINTS

STAPLER

3 DRINKING STRAWS

CUT PAPER IN HALF

DECORATE WITH DESIGNS

DRINKING STRAWS

ROLL AND STAPLE TO MAKE TEPEE

CUT A SLIT AND FOLD FLAPS BACK

COVERED WAGON

Paper people and mules can be colored and cut out of construction paper or lightweight white cardboard. Make a wagon train, several wagons long, and bring them together in a circle at night.

Cut out a wagon bed from brown paper. Cut slits as shown. Fold the sides up and glue. Cut out a top for the wagon from white paper. Glue the sides to the wagon inside the wagon bed.

Cut out four wagon wheels from lightweight cardboard. Color with markers or paint. Glue to the sides of the wagon base. If you want movable wheels, you can use brads to fasten the wheels to the wagon, inserting the brads through the wheel's center and the wagon.

To create a wagon seat, cut a brown paper rectangle and fold. Glue in place. Punch two holes in the front of the wagon bed and insert the yarn.

You can decorate the wagon with barrels made from rolls of paper, yarn ropes, and written messages, such as "California or Bust!"

MATERIALS

- SCISSORS
- CONSTRUCTION PAPER: BROWN AND WHITE
- WHITE GLUE
- TAGBOARD OR LIGHTWEIGHT WHITE CARDBOARD
- MARKERS OR PAINT
- BRADS
- PAPER PUNCH
- YARN SCRAPS

WAGON BED

CUT ALONG DOTTED LINES

FOLD AND GLUE FLAPS TO MAKE A BOX

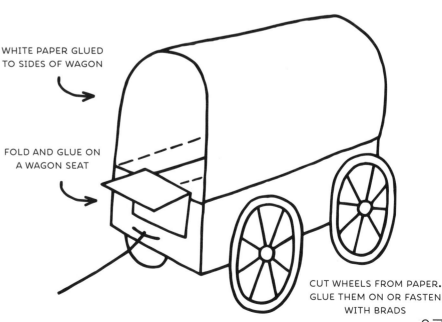

WHITE PAPER GLUED TO SIDES OF WAGON

FOLD AND GLUE ON A WAGON SEAT

CUT WHEELS FROM PAPER. GLUE THEM ON OR FASTEN WITH BRADS

27

WINTER COUNT

The Native Americans in the West didn't write to each other with quill pens. They used hides and homemade dyes to communicate their important thoughts. Winter counts were an important part of Native American life. A winter count was made on a large tanned animal hide. Each year important events were drawn on the hide. These records showed what had happened over several winters' time. They were handed down through the years and are a valuable record of life in those days.

You can make your winter count from a grocery bag. Cut the bag apart at the seams and smooth it out flat. Tear all the edges away, giving the bag a rough shape, like an animal skin.

Using the markers, draw events in your life. Start with your birth and record all the important things that have happened to you by drawing pictures to represent each event. It's easy to show family births, moves, new schools, and hobbies.

To store your winter count, roll it up and tie with a piece of yarn.

MATERIALS

BROWN PAPER
GROCERY BAG

MARKERS OF
ASSORTED COLORS

ROLLED PAPER BEADS

You may want to wear a colorful bead necklace as you write your winter count.

Cut triangle shapes from some magazine pages. Small triangles make smaller beads, larger triangles make larger beads. Experiment a little, trying several sizes to make your necklace interesting.

Roll the paper triangle over a pencil with the wide end down first. As the point rolls up over the broad side of the paper, rub a little glue under the pointed end. Roll tight. Hold it firmly for a few seconds to be sure the glue will stick. Then slide the bead off the pencil.

Make a pile of beads, and then begin stringing them on the string. Colorful yarn looks fine; dental floss is very sturdy. Tie a knot with the ends and wear with pride!

MATERIALS

COLORED PAGES FROM MAGAZINES

PENCIL

WHITE GLUE

STRING

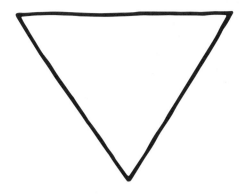

CUT TRIANGLES FROM MAGAZINE PAGES

ROLL UP AND GLUE

WHEN DRY, STRING ON YARN

SILVER & TURQUOISE BRACELETS

Native Americans in the Southwest love to make and wear beautiful silver and turquoise jewelry. You can, too!

Using scissors, cut the toilet tissue tube apart down one side. Then cut off a section about 1 1/2 inches wide. Trim the corners so they are slightly rounded as shown.

Using a strip of aluminum foil twice as big as the section of paper tube, cover the tube section with the foil, shiny side out. Smooth the foil and press the edges to the inside of the tube section. This is your silver bracelet.

Now, color the macaroni to represent turquoise stones found in the desert of the Southwest. Fill a cup with 1/2 cup of rubbing alcohol. (Alcohol dries and evaporates more quickly than water, but you can use water.) Tint the alcohol with several drops of blue food coloring. Drop macaroni seashells into the alcohol and let them set until they are dyed a bright blue. This takes about 10 minutes. Place the macaroni on a plate and let dry.

When the "stones" are dry, glue them onto the bracelet with dabs of white glue. Make any designs you wish.

MATERIALS

SCISSORS

EMPTY TOILET TISSUE TUBE

ALUMINUM FOIL

SMALL SEASHELL MACARONI

RUBBING ALCOHOL OR WATER

BLUE FOOD COLORING

WHITE GLUE

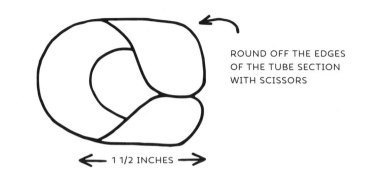

ROUND OFF THE EDGES OF THE TUBE SECTION WITH SCISSORS

1 1/2 INCHES

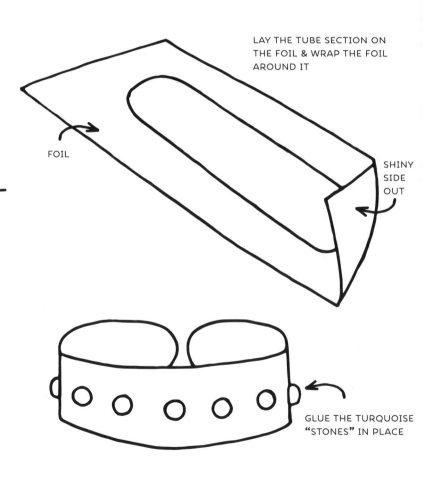

LAY THE TUBE SECTION ON THE FOIL & WRAP THE FOIL AROUND IT

FOIL

SHINY SIDE OUT

GLUE THE TURQUOISE "STONES" IN PLACE

CLAY AND DOUGH

CLAY IS SUCH A GREAT MEDIUM— IT'S NOT EXPENSIVE, NOT TOO MESSY, AND TAKES FEW SUPPLIES.

Children of all ages love to work with it. Projects turn out so shiny and "real." Best of all, it's a very expressive medium; most children derive real satisfaction from both the process and the end result. An added benefit is that pinch pots and other ceramics make great paper clip holders or tiny vases for a bouquet of violets. Imagine how pleased a young potter will be to see his or her work of art being used and displayed!

Pottery clay can be purchased at art supply stores, some paint stores, and through any ceramic shop. It often comes in 25-pound blocks that will make about fifty small dishes or pots. The clay will need to be fired if you want the pottery to be permanent. In order to adequately fire it at the necessary temperature, you will have to use a kiln. While few of us have ready access to a kiln, most local ceramic shops will fire projects for you, charging a small amount for each piece fired. Be sure to make firing arrangements before you buy your clay.

There are three ways to build pots or dishes from clay. Slab, coil-built, and pinch are easy enough for children of all ages to do. The secret to a successful clay piece is to "pull" the piece into shape using the tips of your fingers to shape. Avoid patching small pieces of clay together. Also, be careful that you don't pinch the edges of your object so thin that they crack while drying or firing.

DRYING & FIRING

No matter what type of clay project you do, you must allow the finished item to dry thoroughly. This can take at least a week to ten days. Test for dryness by holding the pot to your cheek. If it feels cold, it is not completely dry.

If you fire clay items that aren't dry inside, the high temperatures of firing cause the internal clay molecules to explode. If your pot explodes during firing, not only will that pot be ruined, but the flying bits of pottery within the kiln will break other items being fired and can cause serious damage to the inside of the kiln. Don't be overanxious to get something fired. You can hurry drying time along by placing the items in a warm spot, like near a stove, on top of a water heater, or near a heating vent. Direct sunlight will dry the items, but if it's too hot, they may dry too fast and crack.

FINISHES

One advantage in using fired clay is the variety of finishing techniques and effects that can be used on the finished object.

The most permanent finish is a ceramic glaze specially formulated to be fired in the kiln. These glazes come in a wide variety of colors and effects, from opaque to transparent. The glaze is painted with a paintbrush on the fired clay object, allowed to dry, and then fired again in the kiln. This sets the glaze permanently so that ceramic dishes hold water and can even be washed in the dishwasher. Never apply glaze to the bottom of a ceramic piece as the glaze will melt the piece to the kiln. In fact, always carefully wipe the bottom edge before firing a glazed piece. Always specify that you want lead-free glaze, safe for eating utensils, when purchasing glaze. These firing glazes can be purchased through any

ceramic shop. Glazes are applied with regular paintbrushes and cleaned up with soap and water.

While glazing is very popular, there are many other ways to finish a fired ceramic piece. Acrylic paints and finishes, sold in art supply stores, work very well. Although they don't need to be fired, they do dry to a waterproof finish. Watercolors and tempera paints can also be brushed on. They will be permanent if the piece is then sprayed with an acrylic spray finish.

One of my favorite techniques for finishing clay pieces is using a soft cloth to rub shoe polish paste over the surface of the clay. It gives the pot a weathered effect and is particularly nice with textured clay surfaces. Use it to finish clay "fossils." This method is inexpensive, quick, and easy to do. When the polish is dry, brush on a coat or two of acrylic floor wax. It will dry to a nice soft sheen. Advantages to using the floor wax include its low cost, availability, and easy cleanup with soap and water. A disadvantage is that it isn't permanent. The finished piece can't be washed again and again. But it is a fine finish to use for clay items that will be displayed such as plaques, paperweights, or sculptures.

A slightly messy finishing method involves painting the fired clay pieces with tempera, drying them, and then dipping the pieces into melted wax. Adults must do the wax finishing process because the wax can ignite at high temperatures. Using a double boiler to melt paraffin, lower the clay piece into the hot wax with a wire strainer. Lift it out gently, letting excess wax drip off. Cool the ceramic piece on a plate covered with wax paper. When cool, it will have a nice sheen. Waxed pieces are very nice to use as Christmas ornaments or display pieces.

Chalking can be done to a finished fired piece. It creates a soft, delicate effect. The fired piece is given a coat of white acrylic paint. When dry, apply chalk pastels with a bristle brush. Scrub the bristles into the chalk and then apply to the desired areas on the clay piece. This technique is used to create natural-looking animal and wildlife sculptures. Once the chalk is applied, give the piece a spray coating of acrylic low-sheen finish.

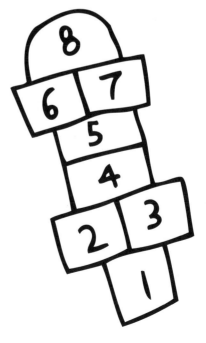

PERFECT PINCH POTS

Take a ball of clay the size of a large orange. Shape it into a pot by first pushing both thumbs together into the middle and shaping it by pulling the sides out from the center. Don't pinch the edges too thin. Build it up and out from the center, giving it the shape you want.

Wet your fingertips in a little water and smooth out any cracks in the surface of the pot.

CLAY PROJECTS

PRESS YOUR THUMB
INTO THE CLAY BALL
TO BEGIN THE POT

SMOOTH ANY CRACKS
ON THE POT

SIMPLE SLAB DISH

A very easy clay dish can be made using the slab method. Use a rolling pin or large wooden dowel to roll the clay out flat and smooth, just like making sugar cookies! Roll the clay out to 1/2 inch thick. Cut a large shape from the slab; a large free-form oval is just fine. Place a damp cloth over a form or mold such as a bowl. Drape the wet clay over it to dry. Allow the clay to dry over the form, and it will retain the molded shape after firing. Most bowls found in the kitchen work very well. You can drape the clay over the upturned base of the bowl as shown or place the damp cloth inside the bowl, and then lay the clay on the inside bottom of the bowl. It might take about a week for the clay to dry on the form before finishing and firing.

WET CLAY

DAMP CLOTH

BOWL

REMOVE WHEN DRY

SUPER SLAB DISH

After you have tried the simple slab dish, or if you are pretty confident of your clay-handling ability, you can try cutting slab projects out and pressing them into a variety of shapes. Depending upon the shape of your base, you can make rectangular dishes or round ones, ovals or squares.

Here's how to do one to get you started. Roll the clay to about 1/2 inch thick. Use a table knife to cut a 4 x 4-inch rectangle. This will be the base of your dish. Cut four sides, each 2 x 4 inches. If you cut out a paper pattern first, you will be sure to have all sides equal.

Join the sides to the base by scoring the edges. Scrape the clay edges with a table knife to rough them up a bit. Moisten the scored edges with a little water and press the edges together. Roll a long, thin clay coil (about the size of a large earthworm) and press it along the inside seam where the edges meet, especially around the corners. Smooth it down with a Popsicle stick or similar tool.

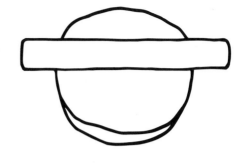

ROLL OUT CLAY TO ABOUT 1/2 INCH THICK

JOIN THE PIECES TOGETHER AT THE EDGES

BASE

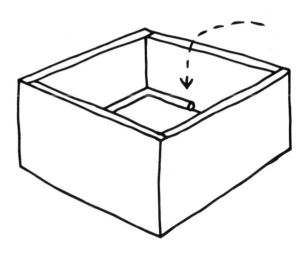

PRESS CLAY COIL ALONG INSIDE SEAM AND SMOOTH WITH A POPSICLE STICK

MOISTEN AND SMOOTH EDGES WITH YOUR FINGERTIPS

COILED POTTERY

Coiled pottery is more sophisticated than slab methods. People throughout history have used the coil method to create beautiful, durable containers.

To get started, make a base by flattening a slab of clay to about 1/2 inch thick. Cut out a round shape from the slab, tracing from a pattern such as a glass or a coffee can with a table knife. Now make several coils by rolling the remaining clay between the palms of both hands, creating a smooth rope of clay. Make each coil about 1/2 inch thick and 12 inches long.

Score the edges of the base with a table fork. Dip a sponge in water and rub over the scoring to moisten it. Place a coil on the top edge of the base and pinch one end flat to the base so that the coil is joined firmly to the pot base. Continue adding coils atop one another, scoring and sponging each coil's surface before winding another above it.

When a coil has been used up, make a diagonal cut at the end of it. Do the opposite to the new coil. Splice them together by scoring, sponging, and applying finger pressure.

When your pot is the size and shape you want, pinch off the end of the last coil, and, using some water and finger pressure, blend the end into the rest of the pot. Continue smoothing the surface of the pot with finger pressure and slight moisture. If you want your pot to hold water, you need to sponge and use finger pressure to smooth the coils together.

Special effects can be created on the surface of your pot by pressing objects into the smooth, wet clay to create textures and repeated patterns. Look for odds and ends such as macaroni, nuts and bolts, bits of heavy lace, pieces of burlap, or whatever you can find.

WIND THE CLAY COIL AROUND
THE TOP EDGE OF THE BASE

USE A MOIST SPONGE AND FINGERTIPS TO
SMOOTH THE COILS FLAT

CLAY FOSSILS

Dinosaur enthusiasts love creating "fossils" from natural objects. Find a few leaves, pebbles, seashells, or even dead bugs for imprinting. Use any kind of soft clay. Your fossils can be air-dried or fired in the kiln.

Roll the clay into a smooth ball then press it flat on the table top. Use a little water to smooth around the outside edges of the clay. Press your chosen object directly into the clay then remove it. Its imprint will remain. If you are satisfied with the quality of the imprint, allow it to dry. If not, roll the clay up and try again.

When the fossil is dry, finish it by rubbing brown shoe polish gently over the surface. Let the shoe polish dry and then brush on a coat of clear acrylic finish or acrylic floor wax, or spray with a clear acrylic spray finish.

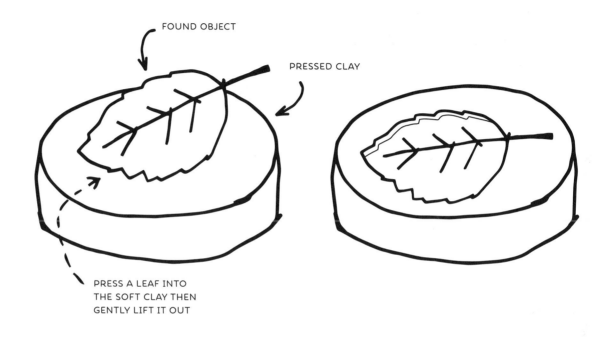

FOUND OBJECT

PRESSED CLAY

PRESS A LEAF INTO THE SOFT CLAY THEN GENTLY LIFT IT OUT

USE LEAVES, SHELLS, OR WHATEVER YOU FIND TO CREATE FOSSILS

MATERIALS

SOFT CLAY

IMPRINTING ITEMS SUCH AS LEAVES, PEBBLES, SHELLS

BROWN SHOE POLISH

ACRYLIC FINISH

FLOWER POCKETS

Flower pockets are easy to make and nice to give as a gift. Roll a slab of clay out to about 1/4-inch thickness. Use a toothpick or pencil to trace an outline on the slab and a table knife to cut it out. Cut a rectangle from the clay about 5 inches wide and 9 inches long. Cut off the corners from one end, creating a rounded edge as shown. Use a drinking straw or a pencil to punch a hole in the rounded end. Moisten the edges of the clay and fold the bottom third of the rectangle up over itself to create a pocket. Press the edges together to seal the clay. Decorate the surface by drawing simple designs or patterns with toothpicks or by pressing pieces of burlap or lace gently into the clay.

Insert a piece of crumpled newspaper into the pocket to keep it open as the piece dries. When completely dry, remove the paper and fire in a kiln. Flower pockets can be glazed, painted, or finished with shoe polish. Stick some dried flowers, weeds, or pods into the pocket. Hang on the wall by the hole, or string some ribbon or yarn through the hole, tie a bow, and hang from the ribbon.

MATERIALS

CLAY

TOOTHPICKS

TABLE KNIFE

STRAW OR PENCIL

NEWSPAPER

GLAZE, PAINT, OR SHOE POLISH

DRIED FLOWERS

RIBBON OR YARN

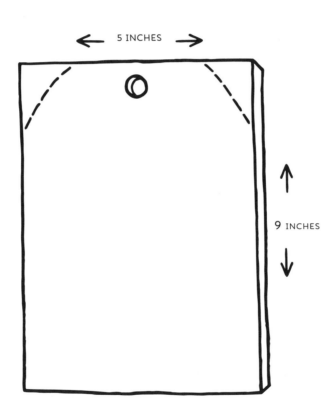

← 5 INCHES →

9 INCHES

ROLL CLAY OUT 1/4 INCH THICK.
CUT AND TRIM
AS SHOWN

FOLD UP TO MAKE A POCKET

AFTER FIRING, FILL WITH DRIED FLOWERS AND HANG FROM A RIBBON

GINGERBREAD SPOON REST

Roll some clay flat to about 1/4-inch thickness. Use a gingerbread boy cookie cutter, or trace around a pattern with a toothpick. Cut out with a table knife. Moisten your fingertips and smooth the cut edges slightly.

Use toothpicks to make eyes, a smile, and buttons in the clay. You can also roll tiny balls of clay, moistening slightly, and press into the surface of the boy to create buttons or decorative trim.

Lay the cut-out gingerbread boy inside a paper bowl or salad bowl to dry. This gives the clay a concave shape, perfect for a spoon rest. When completely dry, fire in a kiln. Finish the piece with a glossy glaze of your choice and fire.

MATERIALS

CLAY

GINGERBREAD BOY
COOKIE CUTTER

TABLE KNIFE

TOOTHPICKS

SMALL BOWL

GLAZE

HAIR BARRETTES

These simple and very special hair barrettes are made from small leftover clay scraps. Use purchased metal barrettes for mounting. Cut or roll the clay into rectangular pieces slightly larger than the metal barrette base. Incise a decorative design on the clay using toothpicks to draw with or nuts, macaroni, or buttons to make prints and patterns. Place the decorated clay piece on a slightly curved surface, such as the underside of an upturned bowl. Let dry. Fire if you choose. Paint or glaze, and then glue to the back of the metal barrette. I use a hot glue gun for this project, but any reliable craft glue works.

MATERIALS

LEFTOVER CLAY

METAL BARRETTES

IMPRINTING MATERIALS SUCH AS TOOTHPICKS, NUTS, MACARONI, OR BUTTONS

GLAZE OR PAINT

GLUE

CLAY PRETTIES

CUT AND DECORATE SMALL CLAY STRIPS

LET DRY ON A CURVED SURFACE

GLUE TO A BARRETTE

LET BEADS DRY ON A STRAW OR SKEWER

BEADS CAN BE MANY SHAPES AND SIZES

BEADS

You can make great beads from your leftover clay scraps. Make them large or small, in any shapes you choose. Stick a drinking straw or long, wide bolt through the middle of each bead, allowing several to dry in place on a straw. If you want a smaller hole in the middle, stick them on a barbecue skewer or nail.

When dry, the beads can be fired or not. Decorate with paint, glaze, or leave them natural. Spray with an acrylic finish. String them on thread, skinny ropes, ribbons, dental floss, or fishing line.

MATERIALS

LEFTOVER CLAY

STRAWS OR BOLTS

PAINTS OR GLAZE

ACRYLIC FINISH

THREAD, SKINNY ROPES, RIBBONS, DENTAL FLOSS, OR FISHING LINE

CLAY BUTTONS

Buttons made from clay look great on sweaters, coats, or almost anything you want to personalize.

Either roll clay into a thin slab and cut out the button shapes, or roll into small balls in your hand and flatten against the table top. Use toothpicks or narrow skewers to punch holes (at least two) in the middle of the buttons.

Use toothpicks to press in a surface design. If you have access to leatherworking tools, tiny designs can be imprinted.

Let the buttons dry, and then fire them. To finish, spray with acrylic or glaze the top surface and fire. Be careful to keep glaze from getting on the underside or the glaze will melt in the kiln and fire the buttons to the kiln's shelf. When fired and glazed, buttons made from ceramic clay can be machine washed and dried on the gentle cycle. It's best to button the garment and turn it inside out first. Keep in mind that clay shrinks when drying and firing. If you are creating a button to fit a particular size buttonhole, make it about 1/3 larger than needed to allow for shrinkage.

MATERIALS

CLAY

TOOTHPICKS

GLAZE OR ACRYLIC

CUT CIRCLES

PUNCH HOLES IN CENTER

PRESS DESIGNS INTO THE MOIST CLAY

SEW BUTTONS ON TO YOUR FAVORITE CLOTHES

41

HOMEMADE CLAYS

SAWDUST CLAY

Few people have used this type of clay, but after I tried it, I loved it! It's very inexpensive, and the results can be quite impressive. When dried in the sun, sawdust clay becomes very hard and can be sanded with sandpaper before it's painted. Children of all ages can use it, cleanup is easy, and one bucket of sawdust will keep you busy for a long time.

To mix the clay, use a large bowl or bucket. Mix 2/3 parts of sawdust and 1/3 part of flour together. Pour in water and mix until it reaches a stiff but "squishy" consistency. Add more flour if it is too crumbly. The clay needs some kneading before the gluten in the flour becomes elastic, holding the sawdust together. Work it in your hands or on a table top covered with newspapers. Play with the clay a little until it becomes easy to shape.

This clay has a thick heavy texture, and the best type of projects seem to be Native American-type pottery pieces. Take large balls of clay. Push your thumbs together into the center, shaping the sides as you go for bowls and other containers. Sawdust clay can also be rolled flat and cut into shapes with cookie cutters. Poke a hole in each cut-out with a drinking straw. When dry, string with yarn to make simple wall decorations or Christmas tree ornaments.

This clay air-dries very hard. It should be placed directly in the sun, if possible. When dry, you can sand it or not, depending upon what you like. Use tempera or acrylic paints to decorate the finished objects. To give your pieces a glossy coating, spray with acrylic clear finish or paint with acrylic floor wax.

MATERIALS

LARGE BOWL OR BUCKET	1/3 PART FLOUR
2/3 PARTS FINE SAWDUST (ANY KIND EXCEPT REDWOOD)	WATER

CERAMIC & POTTERY CLAYS ARE A LOT OF FUN, BUT YOU AREN'T LIMITED TO THEM. THERE ARE SEVERAL KINDS OF CLAY & DOUGH YOU CAN CREATE YOURSELF FROM INEXPENSIVE MATERIALS.

SAWDUST

SAWDUST

FLOUR

BREAD CLAY

This clay is nice for making small, delicate ornaments and figurines. You can also make flowers, forming each petal by rolling and pressing the clay into shape.

To create bread clay, remove the bread crusts and break the bread into small pieces. Add the glue—1 tablespoon of white glue per 1 slice of bread. Mix with a spoon, then knead with your fingers until it's soft and pliable. If you want to work with a colored dough, add a small amount of tempera paint to the clay. Knead it to spread the color evenly. This clay can also be tinted by mixing food coloring with the white glue before mixing with the bread.

To detail the clay figures, use your fingernails or toothpicks. When the figurines are finished, glaze with a mixture of equal parts water and white glue to prevent cracking or shrinking as the clay dries. After the pieces are air-dried, they can be painted with acrylics, tempera, or given a rubbed finish with shoe polish paste.

This clay keeps several days in the refrigerator if well sealed.

MATERIALS

DRY, STALE WHITE BREAD

WHITE GLUE

SALT DOUGH

There are many recipes for salt dough. Some require cooking, some don't. Some have a stiffer texture, just right for creating small details. Others are softer, ideal for young hands. All are inexpensive and store well when wrapped tightly or stored in an airtight container in the refrigerator. Salt dough can also be frozen and thawed for use later. Choose your favorite from the five recipes on pages 44 and 45.

Food coloring is usually recommended to color the various doughs. Liquid or powder tempera paint also works. If you use plenty of coloring, you don't have to paint the surface of the finished object. Simply spray it with clear acrylic sealer. Brightly colored dough looks better than faded, weaker colors once the dough dries. Paste food coloring sold with cake decorating supplies gives a more intense color, so you may choose to use that instead of the liquid variety.

Use wax paper as a working surface and also to air-dry dough products. Work on foil-covered cookie sheets for projects that must be baked in the oven.

If you are making a hanging ornament, small pieces of twisted wire or paper clips can be inserted into the dough before it hardens. Otherwise, remember to make a hole with a straw or nail before the dough hardens.

Salt dough is good for molding. Use gelatin molds, candy molds, or marzipan molds. Dust the mold's surface lightly with cornstarch or flour before pressing dough in place.

A variety of tools can be used with salt dough. Search your garage tool box and kitchen drawers for picks, nails, Popsicle sticks, bottle caps, tweezers, golf tees, or cookie cutters. Melon ball cutters and pastry wheels are also useful.

The most fun and versatile tool is a garlic press. Use it to squeeze out tiny noodles of dough to create hair, beards, grass, or manes. Inexpensive garlic presses can be found in a supermarket or kitchen store.

A GARLIC PRESS MAKES SALT DOUGH INTO TINY NOODLES FOR HAIR, GRASS, OR MANES.

SALT DOUGH 1

Measure the cornstarch and baking soda into a saucepan. Mix and add 2 1/2 cups of cold water. Place on medium heat. Stir for about 5 minutes until the mixture thickens. Remove from the heat. Cover the pan with a wet paper towel. When cool, knead for about 5 minutes, working on a surface covered with wax paper.

Allow objects to air-dry before painting.

MATERIALS

2 CUPS CORNSTARCH

4 CUPS BAKING SODA

2 1/2 CUPS COLD WATER

SALT DOUGH 2

Bring the water to a boil in a saucepan. Remove from the heat and stir in the salt. Mix the flours together in a large bowl. Add the salt water to the flours and stir. Knead on a flour-covered surface.

Bake finished objects on a cookie sheet at 250° F for 2–3 hours. Check your objects every 20 minutes after the first 2 hours of baking.

When cool, decorate with tempera, acrylic, or colored markers. Spray with clear acrylic finish to protect and preserve.

MATERIALS

2 1/4 CUPS WATER

2 CUPS SALT

3 CUPS WHITE FLOUR

1 CUP WHOLE-WHEAT FLOUR

SALT DOUGH 3

Mix the flour and salt in a large bowl. Add warm water slowly, using your hands to mix all together. Wear rubber gloves if you wish, as the salt tends to dry your skin. Knead on a flour-covered surface for about 10 minutes until the surface is smooth and elastic. Wrap the dough tightly or place in a covered container. Take out only what you will be using for small items. This dough does not keep well, however, so use it as soon as it's made.

If you are making a large object, avoid having dough several inches thick as it will not cook evenly. You can build an armature to support a project by crumpling aluminum foil and building up your dough over it.

Bake thin objects about 30 minutes at 350° F. Larger objects require an hour or more, so set the oven at 300° F or 325° F. Cover any areas that brown before the object is completely baked with pieces of aluminum foil to prevent darkening.

MATERIALS

4 CUPS FLOUR

1 CUP SALT

1 1/2 CUPS WARM WATER

THIS RECIPE RESEMBLES EDIBLE DOUGH WHEN BAKED. IT PUFFS UP SLIGHTLY, SOFTENING EDGES AND DETAILS. WHEN BAKED, IT IS A SOFT LIGHT-BROWN COLOR. SEAL IT WITH A CLEAR MATTE FINISH AND YOU CAN MAKE A LOAF OF BREAD THAT LOOKS GOOD ENOUGH TO EAT!

SALT DOUGH 4

Combine all ingredients in a large saucepan. Use a wooden spoon to stir over medium heat. Stir constantly to prevent sticking. The mixture will be soupy for several minutes and then suddenly it will stick together and can be stirred into a ball. When it thickens, remove from heat and continue stirring. Turn the hot ball out onto a floured surface and begin kneading as it cools.

This recipe makes nice soft dough that can be colored brightly with food colors. It keeps in the refrigerator or freezer in a covered container. Use it to play around with or to make small objects which can be air-dried until hard. When dry, they can be painted and sprayed with an acrylic sealer.

MATERIALS

1 CUP FLOUR

1 TABLESPOON SALAD OIL

1 CUP WATER

1/2 CUP SALT

2 TEASPOONS CREAM OF TARTAR

FOOD COLORING

SALT DOUGH 5

Stirring constantly to prevent burning, combine all ingredients together in a saucepan over low heat. In 2 or 3 minutes, it will thicken and can no longer be stirred. Turn out onto wax paper or aluminum foil and cool. When cool, knead until smooth. If the dough dries out, add some water. This recipe makes nice ornaments that are rolled and cut with cookie cutters or designed freehand. Allow to air-dry.

MATERIALS

1 CUP SALT

1/2 CUP CORNSTARCH

3/4 CUP COLD WATER

NUTSHELL ORNAMENTS

Cool and paint with acrylic or tempera paints if you wish. Seal with an acrylic spray coating.

MATERIALS

SALT DOUGH 3 (PAGE 44)

WALNUT SHELLS

TOOTHPICKS

PAPER CLIPS

PAINT

ACRYLIC SPRAY

Use the Salt Dough 3 recipe. This dough doesn't keep well, so only make the amount you plan to use in one session. You need a half of a walnut shell for each ornament or dollhouse creature. Pinch small bits of dough to create a sleeping mouse, baby, or any creature you like.

First, fill the shell with a ball of dough. Then moisten and press a tiny head to the ball in the shell. Create facial features with a toothpick. For a blanket, place a thin piece of dough across the shell and tuck in at the edges. Insert a paper clip or small piece of bent wire into the top of the head for hanging or leave as is for a small treasure. Cover the walnut shell with a small piece of aluminum foil so it won't brown in the oven. Bake at 225° F for about 4 hours.

CLAY TABLETS

This project copies ancient clay tablets that were inscribed with sharp tools. The ancient cuneiform characters of the Assyrians are an example. This project is also a lot of fun for religious school classes, as the tablets given to Moses on Mount Sinai can be duplicated.

Use any of the salt dough recipes, except 3. Roll a ball of dough out flat with a rolling pin and cut it into your tablet shape. Press letters into the surface to create your message. Small toy letters can be purchased in toy departments and are good for small hands to use. Older children can use the alphabet pasta found in grocery stores. Use a toothpick tip to lift the pasta up from the clay after printing. Children may want to draw a picture story or use letters from the Greek or Hebraic alphabets.

Depending upon your recipe, air-dry or oven-bake the tablets. Finish with a light wash of watercolor paint or rub on a little shoe polish. Spray with an acrylic sealer. If you like, glue the tablets to a stained piece of wood and hang on the wall.

ARTS & LETTERS

MATERIALS

SALT DOUGH (NOT 3, PAGES 44–45)

ROLLING PIN

PASTA LETTERS

TOOTHPICKS

WATERCOLORS OR SHOE POLISH

ACRYLIC SEALER

ALPHABET LETTERS

Colorful letters can be made and hung on a bedroom wall. Use any of the baked salt dough recipes. Roll the dough into thick ropes and shape into letters to spell out a special name or word. Moisten edges with water so they stick together when pressed into letter shapes. Tiny teddy bears, fruits, vegetables, or faces can be rolled and shaped from the dough and stuck into position on the letters. Insert a twisted piece of thin wire into the back of each letter before baking so it can be hung on a wall.

After baking and cooling, paint with acrylic paints and spray with a glossy acrylic finish.

MATERIALS

SALT DOUGH (PAGES 44–45)

THIN WIRE

ACRYLIC PAINT

ACRYLIC SEALER

INEDIBLE EDIBLES

CHERRY PIE

PEAS IN A POD

PASTA

It's really fun to create a plate or basket full of fruits, vegetables, and other foods. Glue the food in place on a paper plate to display as a work of art called a still life, or glue magnets to the backs of the individual pieces to use on your refrigerator. Larger pieces can be made to fill a basket or bowl.

Use any of the salt dough recipes (pages 44-45). Color the dough with lots of food coloring so the food will be bright and appealing. Keep each clump of colored dough in a separate container or bag. Two colors can be kneaded together to create another color.

There's no limit to the variety of foods that you can create. I've listed some here, but look in your refrigerator for more ideas!

CHERRY PIE

Roll and cut two triangles from light tan dough. Roll several small balls from bright red dough. Moisten the balls slightly with water and place them on top of one triangle. Be sure they are lined up along the edges. Lay the other triangle on top, creating the top crust of your piece of pie. Crimp the edges together at the wide end of the triangle to simulate a pinched crust. Use your fingers and a bit of water to moisten the edges so they stick together. With a toothpick, prick a few holes in the top of the crust.

PEAS IN A POD

Roll and cut two flat fish-like shapes to create the pods. Roll nine small pea-shaped balls, and moisten each with a little water. Lay five atop one pod and four atop the other. Press the edges of each pod up along the sides to hold the peas in place. Pinch a curved piece and attach as a stem. Press the two pods together at the top, moistening slightly so they stick together.

PASTA

There are two ways to create a dish of pasta—and don't forget, pasta comes in shades of green and red nowadays. If you want it to look like hand-made pasta, roll out some dough to about 1/8-inch thickness. Use a sharp kitchen knife to slice narrow ribbons. Pile the noodles in a dish. If you want a narrower, finer type of pasta, press the dough through your garlic press. For either type, top with a large pat of butter made by rolling yellow dough out and cutting a patty-shape square from it. Moisten the underside of the butter patty and press atop the dish of pasta.

BANANAS

Using yellow dough, roll cylindrical shapes between your palms. Taper both ends and chop the tips off with a sharp knife so they are blunt. When the banana is dry, detail it with brown felt-tip markers. Bananas look best in bunches. Use a little water and pinch them together at the stems so they form a bunch.

CARROT

Using bright orange dough, roll a short fat cylinder for each carrot. By rolling the dough between your palms, you can create a realistic carrot shape that is wide at the top and tapers to a narrow tip. With a paring knife, score the carrot in a few places to resemble the lines on carrots. To add a carrot top, press some bright green dough through a garlic press, moisten slightly, and attach atop each carrot. Carrots look best in bunches of three. Moisten the sides of each so they stick together when dry.

APPLE

Using bright red or yellow-green dough, roll a ball into an apple shape. Push in slightly at the bottom and insert a clove, if you have one, to resemble the stem at the base of an apple. Roll a tiny bit of brown dough and insert at the top for a stem. You may be able to use another clove as a top stem, depending upon the size of your apple. Is that a worm poking out of a hole in the side of the apple? Make the worm by rolling a tiny rope of white dough or pressing dough through a garlic press. Push a hole in the side of the apple with a skewer or pencil and insert the worm. Moisten the worm slightly so it will stick to the apple. When dry, use a black felt-tip marker to dot tiny eyes on the worm.

FRIED EGG

Roll some white dough out flat, cutting a free-form shape from it for your egg white. Smooth the cut edge with a moistened fingertip so it is rounded. Roll a ball from bright yellow dough to make the egg yolk. Press it lightly against the tabletop to flatten its base. Moisten the base of the yolk and set it on top of the white.

DON'T STOP NOW!

GO AHEAD AND ROLL TINY CLUSTERS OF GRAPES, RADISHES, OR LEMONS. ROLL AND CUT OUT PIECES TO CREATE ARTICHOKES, TACOS, AND FRENCH FRIES. JUST BE SURE TO ALLOW EACH PIECE TO AIR-DRY OR BAKE AS NEEDED. THEN SPRAY WITH A SHINY COAT OF ACRYLIC SEALER.

CACTUS GARDEN

The saguaro cactus, with its curving arms, is the type most people think of when they think of a cactus and an easy one to create.

Crumple the foil into an armature to support the soft dough, preventing it from slumping into a glob. Add one or two arms to the base by wrapping another crumpled foil piece around the base piece. Don't crush the foil too much, just enough to give it a cactus shape. It should be about 4 inches tall. To keep your cactus upright, flatten some foil to create a base.

Press a fist-sized piece of dough in place to cover the foil. Smooth the edges of dough pieces with your fingertips so it is smooth. Cover all the foil; don't let any show through. The dough will shrink a little as it dries, so be sure it is least 1/4 inch thick.

Use a dinner fork to indent vertical lines in the dough to look like the ribs on a saguaro cactus.

Break the spaghetti into pieces about 3/4 inch long. Stick the pieces into the soft dough so it looks as if the cactus is covered with spines.

Let dry for 24–36 hours.

A barrel cactus is simpler. Follow the same procedure as the saguaro, but use a foil armature shaped like a pear. Place small pear shapes at the base of the larger one, as they grow in clusters.

To create a nice effect, place the cacti on a small dish and put some sand and pebbles around them. Use craft glue to stick on some colorful strawflower blossoms. Now you have a desert dish garden!

CRUSH FOIL TO CREATE BASE

PRESS IN RIBS WITH A FORK

STICK BROKEN SPAGHETTI IN CACTUS TO CREATE SPINES

MATERIALS

ALUMINUM FOIL (TEAR ONE 10-INCH PIECE FOR EACH CACTUS)

SALT DOUGH 4 (PAGE 45), TINTED BRIGHT YELLOW-GREEN

DINNER FORK

UNCOOKED SPAGHETTI (LONG THIN NOODLES)

PAPER PLATE BASE TO WORK AND TO DISPLAY THE CACTUS ON

MISCHIEF MOUSE

Crumple the aluminum foil into a ball about the size of a golf ball. Roll or press the dough out flat, about 1/2 inch thick. Cover the foil ball with the dough, smoothing the surface of the dough as you cover the foil. Shape the clay like a pear with a flat bottom so the mouse will sit up.

Roll two tiny balls and flatten with your finger tip to create ears. Moisten and attach at the sides of the head. Roll a smaller ball for a nose; moisten and attach. Use a sharp pencil to poke eyes into the dough. Press the side of a straw's opening into the dough beneath the nose to create a tiny smile. Stick some broomstraws or toothpicks about 2-3 inches long into the dough to make whiskers.

Use a straight pin to prick tiny holes all over the surface to allow air to escape during baking. Prick about 1 inch apart all over the mouse's body.

Using a paintbrush, brush a thin coat of milk all over the mouse before baking.

Bake at 350° F for about 45 minutes. When cool, paint inside the ears and the nose. Use a fine-point marker to dot in the eyes. Seal with a clear coat of acrylic. Cut a 6-inch length of yarn for the tail. Use glue to attach the tail to the underside of the mouse body.

MATERIALS

ALUMINUM FOIL

SALT DOUGH (PREPARE ONE OF THE RECIPES THAT REQUIRES OVEN BAKING, PAGES 44-45)

BROOMSTRAWS OR TOOTHPICKS

PIN

PAINTBRUSH

1/4 CUP MILK

MARKERS OR PAINT FOR DETAILS

6-INCH LENGTH OF YARN

GLUE

JAR TOPPERS

Decorated dough-covered jar lids turn a plain pickle jar into a great gift idea. After the lids are baked, glue on candies, tiny decorations such as nutshell animals (see this chapter), toys, or even dog biscuits, if the gift happens to be for your favorite pet.

The recipe for Salt Dough 2 makes enough to cover 6–9 jar lids.

Knead the dough until elastic. Divide into balls, one for each jar lid. Shape each ball over a jar lid.

Use a knife, spoon, fork, or toothpick to make a design of holes and cuts on the dough. This is decorative and also allows air to escape as the lid bakes.

Shapes can be formed from the remaining dough and stuck onto the covered lid. Moisten the dough slightly so the shapes stick better.

Place the dough-covered lids on a cookie sheet. Bake in the oven at 250° F for 2—3 hours or until hard and dry.

Cool.

Decorate the lids with paint or markers. Glue on candies or candy sprinkles. Spray with a clear acrylic coating.

Fill the jars with goodies and gently screw on the lids. Tie a festive ribbon around each jar, and give to a favorite person.

MATERIALS

SALT DOUGH 2 (PAGE 44)

ASSORTED GLASS JARS WITH METAL LIDS

PAINT OR MARKERS

GLUE

CANDIES OR SPRINKLES

CLEAR ACRYLIC SPRAY

PRINT MAKING

PART OF THE FUN OF PRINTMAKING IS GETTING TO CREATE SEVERAL COPIES OF YOUR IMAGE.

Prints make great greeting cards, gift wrap, decorations, or gifts themselves. When considering images to use for printmaking, pick one that is simple and clearly understood. Prints are most successful when there is little detail. Leave out all the little decorative lines. In the process of printing and repeating your design, details do not show up clearly and tend to make the print look fuzzy or messy.

Some printing projects require the use of brayers to pull the ink across a screen or other special equipment and inks. Those are interesting projects for older children or for times when an adult can help with setting up and cleaning up the work area. For other projects, washable inks are available. Acrylic paints or tempera paints can usually be substituted for colored inks.

Let's start with some simpler projects first.

FINGER PAINTING

Use finger paints, painting either directly on a work tabletop or onto a cookie sheet. Using one color or several, move the paint around with your fingers until you have something you'd like to print. Lay a piece of white paper over the painted area and rub the top of the paper lightly. Peel away gently and let dry.

Finger paint prints can be used as a background for drawing or painting, or you can print over a drawing done with colored chalk or crayon, giving it an unusual effect.

MATERIALS

FINGER PAINTS

WHITE PAPER

FINGER PRINTS

THUMMIES

Thummies are so easy to do, and you can continually come up with more ideas for them. Once you start, it's hard to stop!

If using an ink pad, simply press your thumb into the inked pad, and then press it onto paper. Using a marker, add details and background to the print to create an animal, person, or whatever strikes your fancy. If you are using tempera paint, pour a small amount into a jar lid or onto a Styrofoam plate. You may need to gently wipe some off your fingertip before printing.

Thummies make great decorations for greeting cards, stationery, and gift tags. They are a great way to illustrate a story or an experience. Thummies enjoy each other's company, and the more of them you put into a picture, the more fun it becomes.

MATERIALS

INK PAD OR TEMPERA PAINT

PAPER

FINE POINT FELT-TIP MARKER

FOOD PRINTING

If you get artist's block and can't think of a great idea to work on, look in the refrigerator! Fruits, vegetables, and even fish offer tremendous printing possibilities.

Potatoes are easy to work with and don't cost very much. Cut a potato in half and use a toothpick to etch a design into the freshly cut area. Use a paring knife to cut away potato that you don't want in the design. Dip the cut edge of the potato into tempera paint, and press onto paper or cloth. Cutting simple shapes from the potato and then printing them in a pattern on the paper is very effective. Repeating the same shape but using a variety of colors is another possibility.

Other foods that are fun to use are as follows:

Radishes. Cut lengthwise. Leave the greens on and dip them in green paint. Dip the radish in red paint and press onto paper, cloth, or even a T-shirt.

Lemons, limes, grapefruit. Cut crosswise.

Corn-on-the-cob. Roll in paint then roll across the paper.

Mushrooms. Cut crosswise.

Cucumber. Cut in slices and cut designs into the flesh.

Apples. Slice in half either lengthwise or crosswise. When you cut lengthwise, they print red heart shapes or red apple shapes onto paper. Cut crosswise and they leave an unusual star pattern in the center.

Fish, kept frozen or chilled. Fish print best if ink is used, but tempera paints can be used as well. Lay the fish on newspaper or paper towels. Paint the surface with inks and gently lay a lightweight paper over the fish. Press lightly to imprint the fish onto the paper. Peel away and let dry. Use carrot or celery tops dipped in green paint to print plant shapes for your fish to hide in or swim behind.

MATERIALS

FRUIT, VEGETABLES, OR FISH

KNIFE

TOOTHPICK

TEMPERA PAINT

PAPER OR CLOTH

SPONGE PRINTING

Pour paint into the dishes so it is easy to dip the sponges. Use scissors to cut the sponges into simple shapes: stars, hearts, trees, flowers, animals, letters of the alphabet, or whatever else you can think of. Pieces of sponge or foam can be torn into unusual shapes, too.

Dip one side of the sponge into the paint and press firmly onto your paper. Lift the sponge straight off the paper. Sponge printing is especially effective when you repeat the images several times. You can use it to create greeting cards, gift wrap paper, pictures, picture frames, or even to decorate T-shirts. Use like a stencil to decorate your bedroom walls! Use acrylic paints if you choose to paint on fabric or walls so it is waterproof.

MATERIALS

TEMPERA PAINTS

DISHES FOR PAINT

SPONGES: ANY KIND WILL DO LOOK FOR COSMETIC OR KITCHEN SPONGES, PIECES OF FOAM IN A VARIETY OF SHAPES & TEXTURES.

SCISSORS

PAPER

SPONGE ART

CREATE SHAPES FOR PRINTING
FROM SPONGES

APPLE TREE PRINT

Use the brush and brown paint to paint a tree trunk with extended branches on the paper. Dip the sponge pieces into green and gold paint to daub leaf shapes onto the branches.

Dip the cut edge of the apple into the red paint, and print apples among the leaves and branches.

MATERIALS

WHITE CONSTRUCTION PAPER: 1 (18 X 24-INCH) PIECE

PAINTBRUSH

TEMPERA PAINT: RED, GREEN, GOLD, BROWN

DISHES TO HOLD PAINT

SPONGE PIECES: TEAR INTO 1 X 2-INCH IRREGULAR PIECES

SMALL APPLE. CUT IN HALF LENGTHWISE, LEAVING STEM ON ONE PIECE

SANDPAPER PRINTS

With this type of printing, children can create colorful prints that resemble the vivid work of the impressionist artists. Don't try to achieve any detail in the finished picture.

Using bright, vibrant colored crayons, press firmly while coloring a design onto the sandpaper. Try to get as much crayon onto the sandpaper as possible. Lay down several layers of newspapers. Place the sandpaper piece on the newspapers, face up. Cover the sandpaper with the white paper. Iron on top of the paper lightly, at low heat, until the crayon just melts. Remove the paper. Let cool.

MATERIALS

CRAYONS

SANDPAPER (SHEETS OR USED SANDER BELTS CAN BE CUT INTO SMALLER PIECES)

NEWSPAPER

WHITE CONSTRUCTION PAPER

STEAM IRON

ART IMPRESSIONS

COLOR A DESIGN ONTO SANDPAPER

WARM IRON

WHITE PAPER FOR PRINTING

NEWSPAPERS

THE DESIGN WILL MELT ONTO THE WHITE PAPER

BLOCK PRINTS

Use the flat lid of the egg carton. Cut off the edges so you have a flat rectangle. Draw a design on the surface by pressing into the lid with a blunt pencil or ballpoint pen, etching the pencil line into the lid. This technique is called intaglio.

Ink the surface of the lid with the brayer. Lay the paper over the inked piece and rub the paper firmly so it picks up the inked design. Reink the design piece and print again; repeat as many times as you wish.

MATERIALS

RECYCLED EGG CARTON

SCISSORS

PENCIL OR BALLPOINT PEN

WATER-BASED INK OR TEMPERA PAINT

TRAY TO POUR INK INTO

BRAYER

CONSTRUCTION PAPER

TEDDY BEAR PRINTS

Trace the teddy bear pattern onto paper and cut out. Trace around the cutout onto the cardboard. Cut out the cardboard outline. Use a ballpoint pen to press into the cardboard, creating lines and details. Any area that is compressed by pushing down with the pen will not print and will show up on the final project as a white line. Use the pen tip to etch in the features.

Glue the cardboard bear shape to the jar lid. The jar lid holds it firm and keeps your fingers out of the ink when printing.

Use the brayer roller to apply ink or paint to the surface of the bear shape. Press down firmly to print on paper or cloth. When paint is dry, use the marker to color in the bow tie.

MATERIALS

BALLPOINT INK PEN

PAPER FOR TRACING

SCISSORS

PIECE OF THICK CARDBOARD SUCH AS FROM BOXES FOUND IN GROCERY STORES

CRAFT GLUE

LARGE JAR LID

BRAYER

BROWN PRINTING INK OR FABRIC PAINT

WHITE PAPER OR FABRIC TO PRINT ON (TEE SHIRT, CURTAINS, PLACEMATS, BOOK COVER, NOTEPAPER, GIFT WRAP—YOU CAN PRINT ON ALMOST ANYTHING)

RED FELT-TIPPED MARKER

TRACE AND CUT BEAR FROM CARDBOARD AND USE A PENCIL POINT TO CUT LINES INTO THE CARDBOARD FOR DETAILS

GLUE BEAR TO A JAR LID TO MAKE PRINTING EASIER

PRINT ON SHIRTS, BAGS, OR NOTEBOOKS USING ACRYLIC PAINTS FOR THESE PROJECTS

RELIEF PRINTS

Use discarded cardboard, tagboard, or gift boxes. First, cut a backing piece of cardboard the size of the picture you want to print. Start with a small piece, about 8 x 10 inches. Trace and cut out a design from another piece of cardboard. Glue it to the cardboard backing. This will be the printing block.

Cover your work area with plenty of newspapers. You can use ink or tempera paints to print images on paper or cloth. Lay your cardboard printing block on the newspapers, with the design side facing up. Apply ink or paint with a brayer roller.

Lay a piece of paper or cloth over the inked block and press gently over the entire surface so the ink will stick. Peel away and let dry.

Practice by printing on pieces of newsprint the first few times. Begin with designs that use only one color of ink. After some experience, you can brush on particular colors in certain areas of your design to create a multicolor print.

MATERIALS

CARDBOARD

SCISSORS

PENCIL

GLUE

NEWSPAPERS

INK OR TEMPERA PAINT

PAPER OR CLOTH TO PRINT ON

BRAYER

TRIM OFF EDGES OF OLD GIFT BOX

CUT OUT A DESIGN FROM ANOTHER PIECE OF CARDBOARD

GLUE THE CUT-OUT DESIGN ONTO THE OTHER PIECE OF CARDBOARD

APPLY INK OR PAINT WITH A BRAYER

SIMPLE SILKSCREEN

STAPLE FABRIC TO A FRAME
THEN SEAL THE EDGES WITH TAPE

Silk screen printing is actually a stencil method of printing. Paint is forced through a piece of stretched mesh fabric that has been prepared with a design, and the paint is printed onto fabric or paper.

Silk screen is a good way to create several prints of the same image. Greeting cards, gift tags, and posters can be easily made this way.

First you need to prepare a screen. You can use silk, nylon, or other mesh material. Special silk screen fabric is available in art supply stores. You can also use nylon stockings or sheer curtain material. A screen is made from a box top with the center cut out or an old picture frame.

Stretch the mesh fabric tight and attach it to the box by stapling. It is important to keep it very tight. Seal all around the edge of the fabric with masking tape. There must be no spaces or holes.

For young children, a simple silk screen can be made by using an embroidery hoop. Just clamp in the nylon and you're ready to go.

Next make the stencil for printing. Trace the size of your screen and cut the stencil paper the same size. Use newsprint for making the stencil. Fold the stencil paper in half and cut a design from the center fold.

The stencil is used under the screen. Be sure it blocks all areas that are not to be printed. Remember that paint will be forced through any openings in the stencil. Make a squeegee with a piece of cardboard by folding it in half and taping it together. Use it

SCREEN

PAINT

STENCIL

PAPER TO
BE PRINTED

NEWSPAPERS

FOLDED CARDBOARD
SQUEEGEE

MAKE THE STENCIL

for pushing the paint through the screen.

Ready to print! Place the paper to be printed on your table (covered with lots of newspapers). Put the stencil on top of the paper. Lay the screen on top of the stencil.

Drop a teaspoon of finger paint on top of the screen at one end. Using the squeegee, pull the paint from one end of the screen to the other, letting it go through the open areas of the stencil. The paint will cause the stencil to adhere to the screen and will print at the same time. The first print may not be exactly as you want it, so practice on newspaper at first.

When you're pleased with your practice prints, try printing on a piece of colored construction paper. One of the best things about silk screening is that you can make many prints of your image.

MATERIALS

NYLON FABRIC

TOP OF BOX OR OLD FRAME

STAPLER

MASKING TAPE

NEWSPRINT

SCISSORS

CARDBOARD SQUEEGEE

CONSTRUCTION PAPER

FINGERPAINT

RUBBER SOLE STAMPS

Here's another technique to create many stamps for little money. Use shoe insoles, the kind sold in the drug store that can be cut to size. They are made from a thin layer of foam with a layer of latex on one side.

Some insoles have fabric backing on one side, but use the smoother latex side for inking. It is also easy to draw your design on the latex side using a ballpoint pen.

Draw your chosen outline and cut out carefully with scissors. You can glue the cutout to a small wooden scrap or block, which will make printing easy and keep your hands clean. If you don't have wooden blocks, use old metal jar lids. Glue the insole cutout to the block or jar lid with rubber cement.

When the cement dries, you are ready to print. Use a regular inked stamp pad.

Some ideas for stamp designs are: trees, hearts, boats, flowers, butterflies, simple letters or short names, or greetings. You might want to try small fish, bunnies, shamrocks, Easter eggs, or faces.

FUN STAMPS

MATERIALS

SHOE INSOLES

BALLPOINT PEN

SCISSORS

GLUE OR RUBBER CEMENT

WOODEN BLOCK OR JAR LID

DRAW A DESIGN ON THE INSOLE WITH INK PEN AND CUT OUT WITH SCISSORS

GLUE THE CUTOUTS TO WOOD BLOCKS OR JAR LID TOPS TO MAKE PRINTING EASIER

CARVED RUBBER STAMPS

Rubber stamps are so much fun, and everyone can use them. They can be made from a wide variety of odds and ends found at home.

Rubber stamps can be made from erasers; the large pink kind are the best. Use an ink pen to draw the outline you wish to print. Then use a craft knife to cut away eraser surface outside the lines. You can use a straight pin to dig out tiny detail areas.

MATERIALS

ERASERS

PEN

CRAFT KNIFE

STRAIGHT PINS

DRAW A DESIGN ON THE ERASER AND CUT AWAY ERASER OUTSIDE OF THE DESIGN

SCULPTURE
PLASTER PROJECTS

PLASTER IS AN INEXPENSIVE AND EASY MEDIUM TO WORK WITH.

It is exciting to use, and it hardens. This is super for crafts, but a problem for sinks and drains. When using plaster, have plenty of newspaper to cover work surfaces and two buckets—one to mix the plaster in and one filled with water for rinsing off spoons and hands. I also keep a roll of paper towels handy. Plaster is not a problem if you don't pour it down the sink or even wash anything off in your sink. Use the bucket, and, when you're finished, toss the water in the bucket into the shrubbery or on the driveway. Just don't wash any of it down the drain.

Plaster of Paris is inexpensive. It can be purchased in craft stores in small amounts or in building supply centers by the hundred-pound sack. It is cheaper to buy it in the large sack, if you have use for the larger quantity.

Keep dry plaster in a covered container. A coffee can or small garbage can is fine. Plaster absorbs moisture and hardens if not kept dry. I like to save milk jugs for mixing up small batches. Cut the top quarter of the jug away with scissors. Then you can toss the jug out when you are finished, saving on cleanup.

Projects are wet when finished, so set out plenty of newspapers to dry them on.

Mixing plaster: There is no need to measure or weigh portions. Use approximately two parts of plaster to one part of water. I do it the easy way: fill the container half full with water (using warm water speeds setting time). Then, using a cup, I sprinkle the surface of the water with plaster. Continue adding plaster by gently sprinkling on the surface. When the plaster stops sinking out of sight into the water, you have added enough. It will start to "island" and float on the surface of the water. At this point, it is a saturated solution and no more plaster is necessary. Stir gently and slowly. Try to keep air bubbles from forming in the plaster. Let the mixture stand until it starts to thicken, and then pour into the molding container you have prepared earlier.

Plaster usually sets up in about 15–20 minutes. Using warm water or a little salt will speed that up. To slow the setting time, add a small amount of vinegar, alcohol, or sugar to the mixture.

WALL PLAQUES

Wall plaques are all-time plaster favorites. They are easy to do and always look good, expressing the artist's mood at the moment. Use a coffee can lid for a base. Pour the thickened plaster into the lid. Press a handprint—or a pet's pawprint—into the almost hard plaster. You can also drop assorted materials into the plaster to create a design or design anything that suits your fancy. Use a toothpick to inscribe a name and date on the plaque.

Before the plaster hardens, insert a large paper clip or a soda can pop-top into the top edge of the plaque so it can be hung on the wall later.

MATERIALS

COFFEE CAN LID

PLASTER OF PARIS

TOOTHPICKS OR PENCIL

DECORATIVE MATERIALS

PAPER CLIP

POURED PLASTER

POUR PLASTER INTO PLASTIC LID

PRINT SOMETHING IN IT, STICK A PAPER CLIP
OR POP-TOP RING IN IT, AND WHEN HARD,
POP THE PLASTER AWAY FROM THE LID

RELIEF SCULPTURE

Press modeling clay into a pie tin, 1/2 inch thick. Use fingertips and tools to inscribe a scene or design. Stick on pieces of clay, or cut into some parts to give the scene three dimensions.

Mix plaster. When it starts to thicken, pour into the pie pan, covering the clay completely. The plaster should be 1-inch thick. Insert a clip for hanging. Let the plaster dry and set twenty- four hours before removing. Gently lift the plaster up from the clay. Use a table knife to gently separate the two. Rub away any tiny bits of clay that cling to the plaster. When the plaque is dry (it will no longer feel cold to the touch), sand rough edges and stain with some paint or shoe polish and buff to a soft shine.

MATERIALS

ONE POUND OF MODELING CLAY (LIKE PLASTILINA)

ALUMINUM PIE TIN

PLASTER OF PARIS

PAPER CLIP

MOLDING WITH PLASTER

Save any plastic bubble-wrap packages that you find. They come on makeup packages and are used for any small items sold on a cardboard backing. (It would be much better for our environment if we didn't use plastics. If you do find these items, please make every effort to recycle them through many projects.) They make interesting molds for plaster. Sometimes you can find one in a shape that suggests an animal; other times, you may need to stretch your imagination. Rub a little oil or petroleum jelly onto the mold to prevent the plaster from sticking and fill the plastic mold to the top with plaster. Insert a bent paper clip into the wet plaster if you want to hang your creation on a wall or Christmas tree. When completely dry, pop the plaster out and save the plastic bubble for another project. Paint an abstract design on your plaster decoration.

It's fun to work with plaster outdoors. Look for soft mud with a variety of animal tracks. Mix and pour your plaster into the tracks. When hardened, lift the plaster piece gently from the mud. At the beach, dig out a small hole in the soft sand. Lay a few sea shells or rocks with barnacles on the bottom and sides of the hole. Pour your mixed plaster into the hole. Remove it when it has set. If you don't like the clinging sand, brush it off gently, but it does give it an interesting texture.

SCULPTURE
PAPIER–MÂCHÉ

PAPIER–MÂCHÉ IS ONE OF THE MOST EXCITING AND LEAST EXPENSIVE SCULPTING MEDIA TO USE.

It can be used to make simple items like bowls or more intricate work, such as jewelry or puppets. You can purchase premixed papier-mâché compounds at craft shops. These mix up instantly when water is added. Or, you can create your own from flour, water, and old newspapers or paper grocery bags.

While papier-mâché is fun to use, it also quite possibly makes the biggest mess of any medium. It can be cleaned up easily with paper towels and water while it is still wet; after it dries, however, it becomes quite stubborn and difficult to clean up. Cover all work areas and project drying areas with layers of newspapers. Working with papier-mâché is the perfect project to do outdoors, and a sunny day helps the projects dry more quickly.

To get started with any papier-mâché project, gather up newspapers and tear into strips, about 1 x 3 inches for most projects. Gather up containers for mixing the gluing mixture and some paper towels for messy hands.

The paper strips are layered and glued to make a strong, laminated surface which dries hard and can then be sanded and painted. If you want to create large animals or sculptures, use a base or frame under the papier-mâché.

A base can be almost anything that supports the paper strips until they are dry. Large shapes can be created by using pieces of wood or dowels and chicken wire. Smaller objects can be formed around wadded paper balls, rolled and tied newspapers, crumpled aluminum foil, cardboard boxes, or inflated balloons. Papier-mâché can also be pressed into a mold which has been greased with petroleum jelly. When the paper strips are dry, pull the sculpture away from the mold.

To make the glue mixture, you can use wallpaper paste or a flour and water mixture. If you choose to use the wallpaper paste, either the premixed variety or the powdered kind works fine. Add water until it's the consistency of creamy gravy. The homemade flour-water paste is convenient to use because it is handy and inexpensive. Just mix it with water in a bowl and begin dipping the paper strips. If you choose to do your project somewhere else, like outdoors or with a group, save a milk jug. Mix the flour and water glue and pour into the jug. Cap it and it will travel well. Then just pour out what you need into an aluminum pie plate. The glue mixture keeps for a few days covered in the refrigerator. After a short time, it begins to smell, so I usually make only what I need for one session.

Papier-mâché projects need several days' drying time between application of layers of strips. The damp projects must be set in an area with good air circulation or they may begin to mold and smell. A warm open area is fine.

Decorating a papier-mâché project is the most fun! You can use any kind of paint and can also glue on sequins, beads, trimmings, or anything you wish. When your painted project is dry, give it a spray of clear acrylic so it will shine. Papier-mâché looks great when finished with bright, shiny acrylic paints. You can also give the finished project a coat or two of flat white latex paint to seal and strengthen, before finishing with watercolors, markers, or tempera paints.

PLANET EARTH

There are many things to make using a balloon as a mold for papier-mâché. A model of our planet looks really nice hanging from a piece of fishing line from a ceiling. Because your balloon probably won't create a perfectly shaped sphere, it is going to be even more scientifically accurate because our planet isn't a perfectly shaped sphere, either.

Blow up the balloon and tie the end closed. Cover the balloon surface with three or four layers of paper strips dipped in the glue mixture. Insert the clip for hanging. Use the drinking glass or mug to support the balloon while you work so it won't roll around on the table. Allow it to dry.

Paint in the continents and oceans with appropriate colors or use small torn pieces of colored tissue paper. Dip the tissue papers in the glue mixture and then layer them in the appropriate places. Use the brown and green colors for continents, and the blue for oceans. You can wad small balls and glue in place for mountain ranges or islands. Then cover with a layer of more tissue pieces. When dry, coat with an acrylic spray and hang with fishing line.

Warning: Young children can swallow deflated balloons. Please supervise carefully.

MATERIALS

BALLOON*

PAPER STRIPS, CUT INTO 1 X 3-INCH PIECES

GLUE MIXTURE (FLOUR AND WATER)

PAPER CLIP

DRINKING GLASS OR MUG

TEMPERA PAINTS

TISSUE PAPER: BRIGHT BLUE, GREEN & BROWN

ACRYLIC SPRAY

FISHING LINE

PASTE PAPER STRIPS OVER A BALLOON AND SET IT IN A GLASS TO KEEP IT FROM ROLLING

WHEN DRY, PAINT AND HANG FROM CEILING WITH FISHING LINE

PAPIER-MÂCHÉ DINOSAURS

Three types of dinosaurs are easy to make using the paper strip technique. All use a balloon for the tummy area, small boxes for the head, and small paper tubes for legs.

Following the drawings, place several layers of paper strips over the blown-up balloon, using glue mixture, and then tape on the neck and head section. When dry, tape on the paper tubes for the legs and tail sections. When they dry, add spines cut from lightweight cardboard. Feet and hands are cut from the cardboard and taped in place. Layer paper strips over the feet and spines until the whole creature is several layers thick. Allow to dry. Glue on odds and ends to create texture and detail. Use buttons for eyes or glue on paper reinforcements for eyes. Teeth can be made by gluing on rice or inserting broken toothpicks into the damp mouth area before the paper strips are dry. Lentils glued over the entire surface of the creature's body create a reptilian skin texture.

Paint the finished dinosaur and add final details. You can glue on toenails cut from lightweight cardboard. I like to trim off part of a red or pink balloon and glue it inside the mouth so it looks like a rubbery tongue.

Give your finished creature a spray coating of clear acrylic gloss to protect it and help preserve it.

See warning, page 69.

MATERIALS

BALLOONS*

SMALL BOXES (LIKE GELATIN BOXES)

PAPER TUBES (FROM TOILET TISSUE OR PAPER WRAP)

PAPER STRIPS, TORN INTO 1 X 3-INCH PIECES

GLUE MIXTURE (FLOUR AND WATER, CONSISTENCY OF THICK GRAVY)

MASKING TAPE

LIGHTWEIGHT CARDBOARD (MILK CARTONS AND CEREAL BOXES ARE GOOD SOURCES)

ODDS AND ENDS FOR TEXTURE LIKE BUTTONS, RICE, LENTILS, TOOTHPICKS, NEWSPAPER

PAINTS: TEMPERA, ACRYLIC, OR LATEX

PAPIER-MÂCHÉ PULP

IT'S EASY TO MAKE A THICK PULP THAT CAN BE MOLDED INTO SHAPES LIKE CLAY OR PRESSED INTO MOLDS, DRIED, AND PAINTED.

TEAR NEWSPAPER OR PULP PAPER EGG CARTONS INTO SMALL PIECES AND SOAK IN WARM WATER FOR SEVERAL HOURS. SQUEEZE THE EXCESS WATER OUT. SPRINKLE DRY WALLPAPER PASTE OVER THE PULP AND KNEAD WITH YOUR HANDS. WORK WITH YOUR FINGERS UNTIL THE PULP BECOMES SMOOTH AND PLIABLE.

THE PULP MÂCHÉ CAN BE USED TO CREATE UNIQUE PUPPET OR DOLL HEADS, SMALL ANIMAL SHAPES, OR ANYTHING THAT CAN BE SHAPED BY HAND. IT CAN ALSO BE PRESSED INTO CANDY MOLDS, OR GELATIN MOLDS THAT HAVE BEEN COVERED WITH PETROLEUM JELLY. PAPIER-MÂCHÉ PULP HAS BEEN USED FOR A LONG TIME AND WAS POPULAR IN THE VICTORIAN ERA WHEN USED TO CREATE CARVED- LOOKING PICTURE FRAMES, VASES, AND SMALL TABLES.

BRONTOSAURUS

TAPE PAPER TUBES AND
ROLLED PAPER CYLINDERS
TO THE BALLOON

TYRANNOSAURUS REX

HEAD IS A GELATIN BOX—CUT
IT ON 3 SIDES & FOLD IN HALF

TAPE A CARDBOARD
STRIP TO HIS BACK

ARMS ARE MADE
FROM ROLLED PAPER

LEGS ARE PAPER
TUBES

FEET ARE CUT FROM
CARDBOARD

ROLLED AND TAPED
PAPER FOR TAIL

STEGOSAURUS

COVER WITH PAPER
STRIPS AND PASTE

FOR A STEGOSAURUS, TAPE CARDBOARD CUT-
OUT ARMOR TO THE DINO'S BODY AND COVER
WITH MORE PASTED STRIPS

71

DINOSAUR EGG

This egg will really hatch! Surprise your friends when the baby dinosaur hidden in the egg pops out.

Blow up the balloon and tie the end securely. Tape one end of the string to the center of the balloon's middle. Wrap it around the balloon once, and let the loose end of the string hang loose. Being careful not to get the loose string covered with strips, cover the entire balloon (including the one wrap of string) with a layer of strips damped with glue mixture. Wrap the hanging string around the balloon again, and let the loose end hang free.

Cover with another layer of strips. Continue until the string is almost used up and the balloon is covered with several layers of string and papier-mâché strips. Leave about 1 inch of string exposed.

Allow the egg to dry. Using a razor blade or sharp knife, cut two slits in the shape of an "x" in the side of the egg. The balloon inside will pop. Insert the tiny dinosaur into the egg, and cover the opening with two or three damp strips. Dry. Then paint the egg with tempera paint.

To hatch the dinosaur egg and release the tiny dinosaur, pull on the tiny piece of string that is left on the surface of the egg. Pull gently on the string and the egg will pop apart into two halves.

See warning, page 69.

MATERIALS

BALLOON*

TAPE

STRING, ABOUT 30 INCHES LONG

NEWSPAPER STRIPS, CUT INTO 1 X 3-INCH PIECES

GLUE MIXTURE

SMALL TOY DINOSAUR OR ONE MADE FROM CLAY

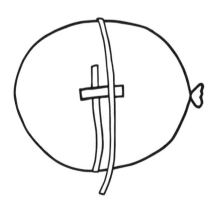

TAPE STRING TO THE BALLOON AND WRAP IT AROUND ONE TIME

PASTE PAPER STRIPS OVER THE STRING LETTING THE LOOSE END HANG FREE

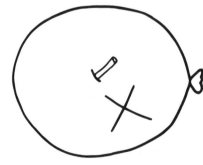

WHEN STRIPS ARE DRY, CUT AN "X" IN THE EGG AND INSERT A DINOSAUR

DINOSAUR BONE

These bones will remind you of the Flintstones! You can make them any size, depending upon the size of your paper tube. If you don't have a large enough tube, make one by taping a large piece of tagboard or lightweight cardboard into a cylinder.

Crush several sheets of newspaper into balls, wrapping crushed sheets with more sheets until they are the size you want. Use masking tape to secure the balls to the ends of the tubes.

Using the torn strips and glue mixture, place three or four layers of strips over the entire bone. Shape the ends while damp, adding more strips as desired to give the ends a bone shape.

Dry and paint with tempera or latex paint. These are really lightweight and make dramatic props for plays, decorations, or Halloween costumes.

TAPE CRUMPLED PAPER BALLS TO BOTH ENDS OF THE TUBE AND COVER WITH PASTED STRIPS OF PAPER

WHEN DRY, PAINT WITH TEMPERA PAINT

MATERIALS

PAPER TUBES (USE PAPER TOWEL ROLLS, TISSUE ROLLS, OR TUBES FROM GIFT WRAP)

NEWSPAPERS

MASKING TAPE

NEWSPAPER OR GROCERY BAG STRIPS CUT INTO 1 X 4–INCH PIECES

GLUE MIXTURE (FLOUR AND WATER, CONSISTENCY OF THICK GRAVY)

TEMPERA PAINT OR LATEX HOUSE PAINT

STUFFED PAPER SCULPTURE

PAPER SCULPTURES ARE LOTS OF FUN BECAUSE THEY ARE BIG, COLORFUL, AND UNIQUE. BEFORE YOU BEGIN, DECIDE WHAT YOU WOULD LIKE TO ENLARGE OR EXAGGERATE. LARGE PAPER FISH ARE EASY TO CREATE. BUT THINK OF WHAT WOULD BE UNUSUAL. HOW ABOUT A LARGE, STUFFED INSECT? CAMERA? EAR OF CORN? WITH A STUFFED PAPER SCULPTURE, THERE IS NO LIMIT TO WHAT YOU CAN CREATE.

Draw the desired shape on the paper and cut out two identical shapes, one for a front, one for the back. Staple the two pieces together until about half the object is stapled. Then begin wadding up newspapers and stuffing the sculpture. Staple the edges as the stuffing fills it up until the entire shape is full and stapled shut. Lay the sculpture on a table top covered with newspapers and begin painting the surface. If you like, use yarn, strips of paper, crepe paper streamers, or whatever you choose to add to your sculpture.

When dry, you can perch your creation on a shelf or tie it on fishing line at the top and hang from your ceiling. These three-dimensional paper sculptures can also be displayed by drilling a hole in a flat piece of wood and inserting a dowel or broomstick. Insert the other end of the dowel into the bottom of the sculpture.

MATERIALS

PENCILS

SCISSORS

BUTCHER PAPER, NEWSPRINT, OR NEWSPAPERS

STAPLER AND STAPLES

NEWSPAPERS (FOR STUFFING THE SCULPTURE)

PAINTS: TEMPERA OR ACRYLICS

OTHER DECORATIONS

DISPLAY BY INSERTING A DOWEL AND STANDING IT IN A BLOCK OF WOOD

STAPLE FRONT TO BACK ALONG EDGES, LEAVING AN OPENING FOR STUFFING WITH CRUMPLED NEWSPAPERS

CRUSHED FOIL SCULPTURE

There are several ways to model with aluminum foil. One way is to model a sculpture out of crushed newspaper shapes and then cover it with aluminum foil. Another way is to use the crushed aluminum foil as a base (or armature) and cover with papier-mâché. Or, you can use aluminum foil alone to create interesting abstract or realistic shapes.

When beginning work with foil, use a piece about 9 x 12 inches to experiment. Work with the foil a bit, crushing, crumpling, pulling apart, and modeling like clay. Tear off small pieces and press back into the surface. Use a pencil point to push in texture and detail.

With foil, you can create recognizable forms such as people, animals, or objects, but you can't create a lot of fine detail. Try to create the general outline or outer contour of the object rather than small areas of detail.

Start with the basic shapes of everyday articles such as fruits, vegetables, chairs, and cars. Then try to make some people in action.

When you have completed your sculpture, cover the cardboard base with aluminum foil and glue the sculpture to the base for display. Use a hot glue gun for quick and secure attachment.

MATERIALS

ALUMINUM FOIL

NEWSPAPERS

CARDBOARD SQUARE: 1 (12 X 12-INCH) PIECE

CRUSH FOIL INTO SHAPES AND PRESS THEM TOGETHER

SMOOTH THE SURFACE AND COVER WITH MORE FOIL

GLUE TO A BASE OF FOIL-COVERED CARDBOARD

WIRE SCULPTURE

LIGHTWEIGHT WIRE: COAT HANGERS, TELEPHONE WIRE, STOVEPIPE WIRE, FINE GAUGE PICTURE-HANGING WIRE

DISPLAY BASES MADE FROM CLAY, WOOD, CORK, CARDBOARD

There are two ways to sculpt with thin wire. One is to create the outside contour or outline of the object, leaving the inner area empty. This is like making a line drawing of the subject.

A more complicated technique begins with the wire silhouette of the object which is then covered with thin wire. Wind the wire in spirals, wrapping it around the form until it is three-dimensional and can stand alone. Then tuck the wire ends inside the body of the sculpture.

After attaching the sculpture to the base with staples or a hot glue gun, the whole thing can be painted with spray enamel. Finished wire sculptures look very dynamic and sophisticated. They make nice gifts to put on a desk or bookcase.

CREATE AN OUTLINE OF THE OBJECT AND GLUE TO A WOOD BASE

TOOTHPICK SCULPTURE

This type of sculpture results in free-form, very modern looking constructions. Any age group will enjoy this project. It is inexpensive and keeps most young sculptors engrossed for quite a while. The gluing is done piece by piece. Allow plenty of time to complete the structure.

Squirt white glue out onto a paper plate. Use the other paper plate as the sculpture's base. Dip the toothpick ends into the glue and arrange them on the plate, building the sculpture upwards. As the glue sets, add more toothpicks, building up in height and width to create a three-dimensional structure. When the glue is dry, spray the entire piece with glossy enamel spray paint; spray the plate as well. This gives the sculpture strength, as well as a finished look.

For a variation, you may want to use drinking straws, cotton swabs (like Q-tips), or coffee stirrer sticks instead of the toothpicks.

DIP TOOTHPICK ENDS IN GLUE AND POSITION THEM IN AN INTERESTING ARRANGEMENT

MATERIALS

WHITE GLUE

TWO PAPER PLATES

TOOTHPICKS (FLAT ONES ARE EASIER TO WORK WITH)

ENAMEL SPRAY PAINT

SOFT SCULPTURE

Young children can make a fabric soft sculpture if an adult is available to help them operate the sewing machine or do the sewing for them. Older children can practice a basic running stitch to sew their own sculptures together.

Any design can be turned into soft sculpture: foods, objects, or animals. You can enlarge items to giant size, like a huge stuffed button or bagel. You can also create wonderful dolls and teddy bears this way.

Fold a piece of fabric in half. Sketch an outline and rough details with pencil on it. Use the markers to outline the shape. Add a 1/4-inch border around the entire shape. This is the seam allowance. Cut out the shape, cutting through both layers of fabric at once. This gives a front and back that are identical and can be sewn together.

Pin the back and front pieces together with the right sides facing each other. Sew around the figure, stitching about 1/4 inch from the edge of the fabric. Leave an opening of 3 or 4 inches for turning and stuffing. Clip the seam allowances at the curved areas so they lie smooth after turning and stuffing. Turn the object right side out and begin stuffing.

Roll the cut edges of fabric to the inside and pin. Using a needle and thread, make small stitches to close the opening. You can also sew the opening shut with a sewing machine.

Finish the sculpture by coloring with markers or paints if you choose. Bits of yarn, fur, feathers, sequins, or whatever else can be glued on to decorate.

MATERIALS

UNBLEACHED MUSLIN, BED SHEETS, OR FABRIC SCRAPS

FELT TIP MARKERS

SCISSORS

STUFFING MATERIALS: POLYFILL, OLD NYLONS, FABRIC SCRAPS

SEWING MACHINE & SUPPLIES

LEAVE AN OPENING FOR TURNING AND STUFFING

CLIP SEAM ALLOWANCES ON CURVED EDGES SO THE SCULPTURE WILL LIE FLAT WHEN TURNED RIGHT SIDE OUT

YARN MAKES GOOD HAIR—GLUE IT ON OR SEW TO THE HEAD WITH A LARGE NEEDLE

TURN, STUFF, AND SEW OPENING CLOSED AND DECORATE AND MAKE CLOTHES FOR YOUR DOLL

SPRING IS HERE

WIND SOCK

Cover the empty container by gluing various colors of construction paper over it. Cut long streamers from the crepe paper or tissue paper and glue them to one open end of the container. Cut out shapes from paper scraps and glue to the outside of the container for decoration.

Punch four holes in the other end of the container, spacing them equally around the rim. Thread string through the holes and double knot. Tie all four strands together at the top. Tie one longer piece of string to the knotted ends and use it to hang your windsock from the edge of a deck, roof, or tree branch.

MATERIALS

EMPTY CARDBOARD ICE CREAM CONTAINER WITH TOP AND BOTTOM CUT OUT

WHITE GLUE

COLORED CONSTRUCTION PAPER

SCISSORS

CREPE PAPER OR TISSUE PAPER

PAPER PUNCH

STRING

ROBIN'S NEST WITH EGGS

Squeeze the yellow-brown dough through the garlic press to create "straw" to build the bird's nest. Shape the straw pieces into a rounded nest.

Roll small lumps of blue dough into egg-shaped balls. Moisten the bottom of each "egg" and stick it into the nest. Let air-dry until hard.

MATERIALS

SALT DOUGH 4 RECIPE (PAGE 45): SOME COLORED YELLOW–BROWN AND LIGHT BLUE

GARLIC PRESS

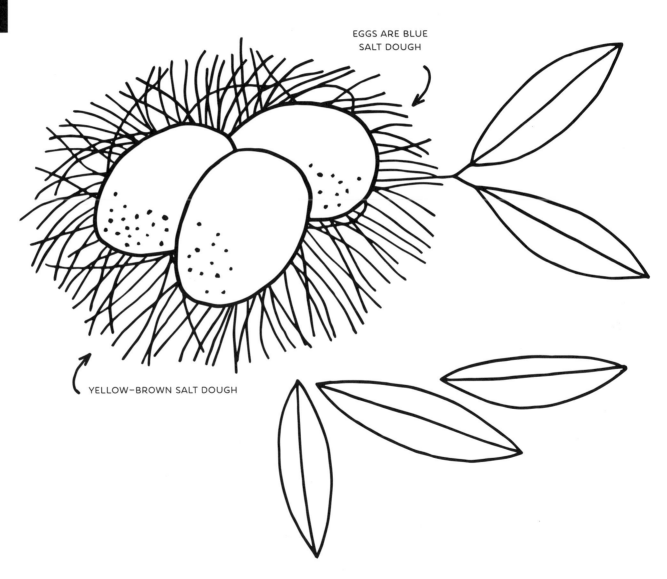

EGGS ARE BLUE SALT DOUGH

YELLOW–BROWN SALT DOUGH

BABY CHICK

You can buy yellow puffs at craft shops or make your own using baby powder and cotton balls. Place a couple of spoonfuls of the yellow powder tempera and a little baby powder into a paper sack. Add 2 cotton balls to the sack and fold the top closed. Shake the balls in the powder. Remove the cotton balls and shake lightly over the open sack.

Glue 1 colored cotton ball in the half eggshell and the other ball on top of the first one.

Punch out 2 black eyes and cut out an orange beak from the colored paper. Glue in place.

MATERIALS

COTTON BALLS

YELLOW POWDER TEMPERA PAINT

BABY POWDER

PAPER SACK

WHITE GLUE

HALF OF AN EGGSHELL, WASHED & DRIED

ORANGE & BLACK CONSTRUCTION PAPER

HOLE PUNCH

SPRING PETS

GLUE EGGSHELL TO A CARD SO IT WILL STAND UP

MOUTH: USE ORANGE PAPER

EYES: CUT OR PUNCH FROM BLACK PAPER

SPRING BUNNIES

For each bunny, cut an 8 1/2 x 11-inch piece of pink construction paper into two pieces, one 5 x 11 inches and the other 3 1/2 x 11 inches. Cut out 2 ears from one end of the smaller strip of paper. Cut out 2 white circles for eyes.

Roll the pink pieces into two loops. Paste or tape to hold the position. Paste the ears in the middle of the 2 loops. Paste the 2 eyes on the smaller loop and a cotton ball on the back of the large loop for a tail.

MATERIALS

SCISSORS

CONSTRUCTION PAPER, WHITE & PINK

PASTE OR TAPE

COTTON BALL

EGGSHELL MOSAIC

Save eggshells until you have enough for a project. Rinse and let them dry. Crush and store them in a container. When you have a couple dozen eggs' worth, make some dye by filling a jar with 1/2 cup of hot water. Add 1 teaspoon of vinegar and a few drops of food coloring. Drop some of the crushed shells into the water. Repeat with other colors of food coloring and more white shell pieces.

Let them soak a few minutes. Spoon them out and allow to dry on a cookie sheet. (Hurry this up by drying on the cookie sheet in a 200° F oven.)

When you have a good assortment of different-colored shells, get your construction paper and glue. Using the cotton swab, paint a design on the paper using the glue. Then sprinkle the colored eggshells onto the glue and shake off the excess.

For variety, you can also use plain white eggshells on colored paper.

EGGSHELL ART

MATERIALS

WHITE EGGSHELLS, RINSED AND DRIED

JAR

HOT WATER

VINEGAR

FOOD COLORING

CONSTRUCTION PAPER

WHITE GLUE

COTTON SWABS (LIKE Q-TIPS)

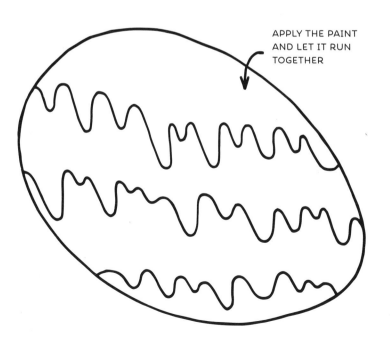

APPLY THE PAINT AND LET IT RUN TOGETHER

GLOSSY EGGS

Cut large white egg shapes out of white construction paper. Mix 4 different colors of food coloring with the condensed milk in 4 separate paint cups. Keep the colors bright and pastel.

Use brushes or cotton swabs to generously paint the eggs in different colors as shown. While the paint is still wet, hang the eggs on a bulletin board with push pins, slanting the egg at an angle. Allow the egg paintings to dry. The paint colors will run together, creating designs that run in a diagonal direction. Allow them to dry for several days until the paint is dry and shines like enamel.

MATERIALS

SCISSORS

WHITE CONSTRUCTION PAPER

FOOD COLORING

SWEETENED CONDENSED MILK (ONE CAN)

PAINTBRUSHES OR COTTON SWABS

PAPIER-MÂCHÉ EASTER EGGS

See the papier-mâché section (pages 67-68) for details on how to use paper strips and a glue mixture. When you have your strips and glue mixture prepared, blow up rounded balloons and knot the ends. Cover the balloons with paper strips and glue. Build up three or more smooth layers of paper. Be sure to cover the knotted end of the balloons. Let dry. Use tempera paints mixed in pastel colors to paint the papier-mâché, decorating in an Easter or spring theme. Or look in a field guide and paint the eggs to look like different bird eggs. When the paint is dry, you can spray the eggs with clear acrylic finish, if desired.

Make a huge basket to hold your giant eggs.

Use brown and green butcher paper. Take about four feet of brown butcher paper, fold it in half lengthwise, twice, and staple the ends together to create a large circle. This will be the basket. To make the bottom of the basket, cut out a circle of brown paper a bit larger that the space made with the sides of the basket. Tape the circle to the inside walls of the basket, forming a bottom. Use another length of brown paper, folded and stapled, to create a handle for the basket. Staple the ends to the sides of the basket. To fill your basket with grass, cut green paper (butcher paper, crepe paper, or tissue) into 1-inch wide strips, and fill the basket with them. Then add your giant papier-mâché eggs to create a real eye-popping display.

See warning, page 69.

MATERIALS

BALLOONS*

NEWSPAPER STRIPS

GLUE MIXTURE (PAGE 68)

TEMPERA PAINTS

ACRYLIC FINISH

BROWN AND GREEN BUTCHER PAPER

STAPLER

TAPE

*SEE WARNING, PAGE 69.

84

PINWHEEL

If using white paper, color or paint a colorful, abstract design. Place design face down. Draw dots on the corners and center of the paper. Cut along the dotted lines as shown, but don't cut all the way through the center of the square.

Fold the corners into the center of the square, lining up the dots on top of each other.

Push the straight pin through the corner dots, through the dot in the center of the square, and into the side of the pencil's eraser. Blow into the pinwheel and watch it spin!

MATERIALS

6-INCH SQUARE PIECE OF PAPER

PAINT

PENCIL WITH ERASER

SCISSORS

STRAIGHT PIN

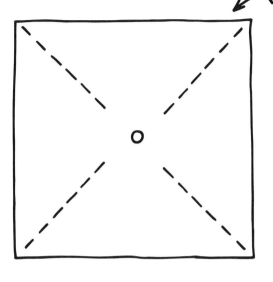

CUT FROM CORNERS ALMOST TO CENTER

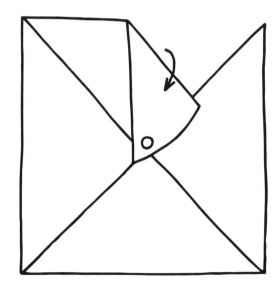

FOLD THE DOTTED CORNERS TO THE MIDDLE

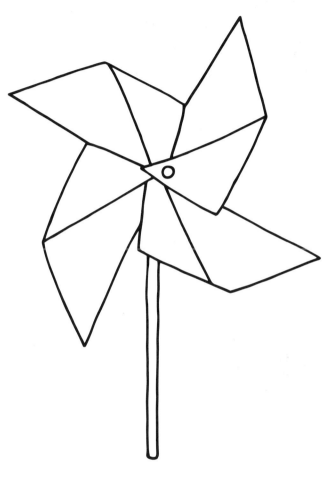

USING A PIN THROUGH THE CENTER, FASTEN THE PINWHEEL TO THE PENCIL ERASER

85

SPRING LILY

Trace the petal pattern onto the printer paper. Cut it out. Fold along the dotted lines to create the flower. Glue the last petal to the first one as shown. Leave the bottom open a bit to allow space for the stem to stick through.

Cut a 1 x 1-inch piece of yellow tissue paper. Glue it to cover one end of the straw.

Cut leaf shapes from the green tissue. Cut 2 strips of green tissue paper, about 1 x 24 inches. Wrap these green strips around the straw, covering it completely. Glue the 2 ends securely.

Insert the covered straw into the base of the flower. Tape or staple in place. Wrap another strip of green tissue to cover the stapled area.

Glue or tape the leaves to the stem.

To give your flower the final touch that makes it really look like a lily, roll the petals around a pencil to give them a curled, natural look. Now make a whole bouquet to fill a vase with springtime.

MATERIALS

PENCIL

CONSTRUCTION OR PRINTER PAPER: COLORED OR WHITE

SCISSORS

GLUE

TISSUE PAPER: A TINY PIECE OF YELLOW, AND 1 (12 X 24-INCH) PIECE OF GREEN

DRINKING STRAW

TAPE OR STAPLER

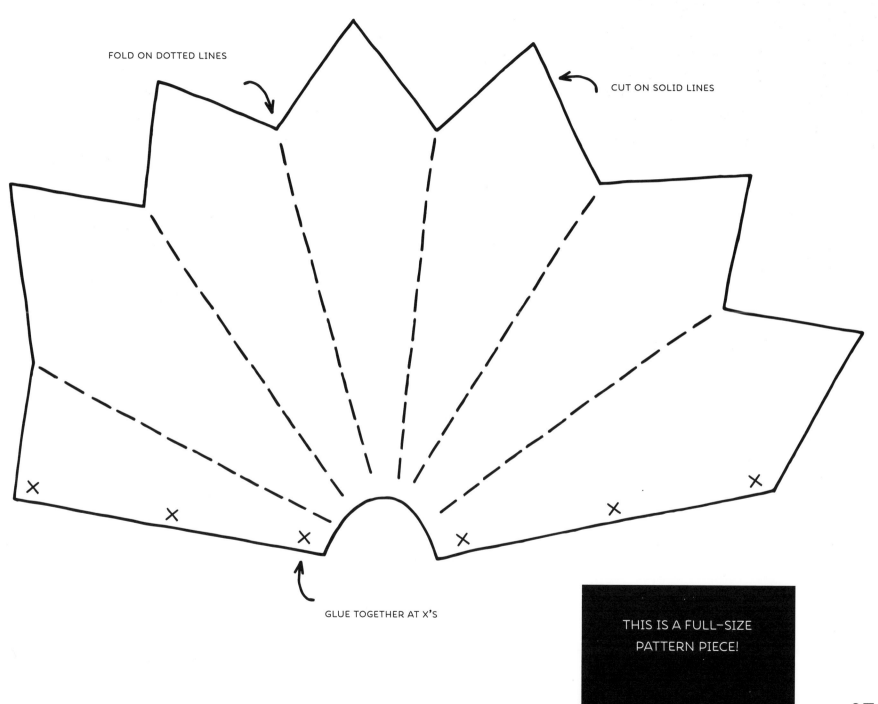

FOLD ON DOTTED LINES

CUT ON SOLID LINES

GLUE TOGETHER AT X'S

THIS IS A FULL-SIZE
PATTERN PIECE!

BIRD IN A CAGE

Blow up the balloon and knot the end. Dip the string in white glue and wrap it around the inflated balloon. Continue wrapping, running the string over other wraps until the string begins to resemble the bars of a cage. Let dry. When the string is completely dry, pop the balloon and pull the pieces out of the string cage.

Draw a bird on the colored paper and cut it out. Punch a hole in the top of the bird shape and hang it by a string inside the cage. Use another piece of string to hang the cage from a tack in the ceiling or on the patio.

*See warning, page 69.

MATERIALS

BALLOON*

STRING

WHITE GLUE

CONSTRUCTION PAPER THE COLOR OF BIRD

PAPER HOLE PUNCH

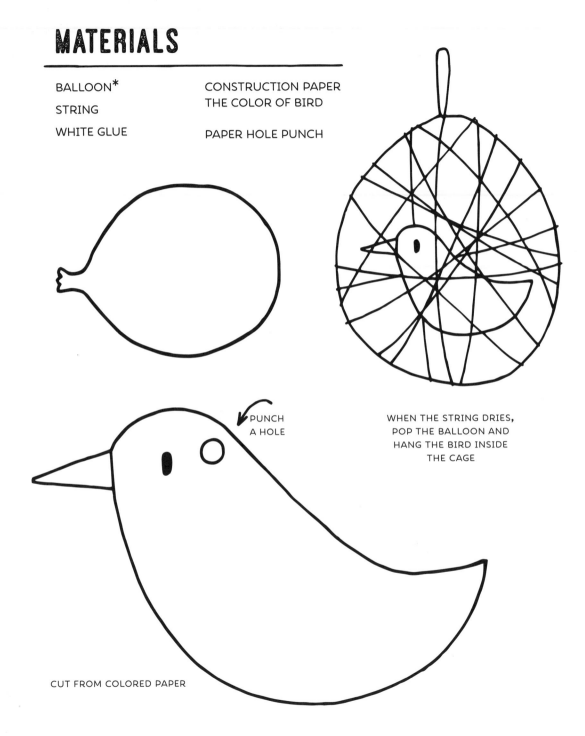

WHEN THE STRING DRIES, POP THE BALLOON AND HANG THE BIRD INSIDE THE CAGE

PUNCH A HOLE

CUT FROM COLORED PAPER

CRAYON COOKIES

Old crayons can be made into giant crayon cookies in different ways. You can melt all the similar colors together, then pour into the paper cupcake liners and cool. Different colors can be layered over one another, letting each layer cool before adding layers of another color, creating two and three colors in one cookie. Or, after the paper liner is about 1/2 inch full of melted crayon wax, drop in broken bits of unmelted crayon. They melt a bit and become part of the solid cookie when it cools.

Another method makes use of an oven. Chop the old crayons up into 1/4-inch pieces and place in the bottom of paper cups. Place the cups in a muffin tin and put in a 400° F oven. Bake until the crayons just start to melt, about 5 minutes.

MATERIALS

OLD PIECES OF CRAYONS, BROKEN UP

PAPER CUPCAKE LINERS

PAPER CUPS

MUFFIN TIN

CRAYON CRAFT

Don't melt the crayons completely or the colors will all mix to form one muddy color. Remove from the oven and cool. Remove the paper when completely cooled. Crayon cookies are fun to use for leaf rubbings or for scratchboard.

WARNING: *CRAYON WAX CAN IGNITE AT HIGH TEMPERATURES, SO BE CAREFUL. ASK AN ADULT TO HELP AND USE A DOUBLE BOILER.*

LAYER DIFFERENT COLORS TO
MAKE RAINBOW CRAYONS

DROP BITS OF CRAYON INTO
THE MELTED CRAYON WAX

CRAYON SCRATCHBOARD

Color the entire piece of board with crayons, putting different colors in different areas. Color firmly, letting no white of the board show. The thicker you apply the crayon, the better your finished work will be. Color over the entire colored board with a black crayon. Color thickly, covering up all of the crayon colors you just applied. Using scratch tools, scratch out a drawing. This is your chance to draw in lots of tiny details with your scratch tool. As the black crayon is scratched away, brilliant colored areas will peek out from beneath it. If you make a mistake while scratching your drawing, just color over it again with the black crayon and scratch again.

MATERIALS

TAGBOARD OR LIGHTWEIGHT CARDBOARD: 8 X 10 INCHES OR SMALLER

CRAYONS OR CRAYON COOKIES (YOU JUST MADE THOSE!)

SCRATCH TOOLS: PAPER CLIP, NAIL, STRAIGHT PIN

POPCORN APPLE BLOSSOMS

With brown paint or markers, draw a large tree branch on the blue paper. Add some green leaves. To create the fluffy apple blossoms, glue on pieces of white popped corn.

MATERIALS

BROWN AND GREEN
TEMPERA PAINT
OR MARKERS

LIGHT BLUE
CONSTRUCTION PAPER

WHITE GLUE

1 CUP POPPED POPCORN

GLUE POPCORN
DOWN FOR
BLOSSOMS

PAPER PLATE BUTTERFLY PUPPET

Draw a large butterfly on the underside of one plate. Use paint or markers to color it in completely with bright designs. With scissors, cut the other paper plate in half. Trim away 1 inch from the cut edges of each half. Fold the plate with the butterfly on it in half. Crease down the center of the butterfly's body. Fold the sides of the plate back toward the butterfly's body. Staple the cut plate halves to back side of the plate with the butterfly on it. Place plates so an opening is created along the crease of the colored plate. To operate the puppet, insert your thumb in one pocket and your fingers in the other. Close your hand and open it. The butterfly will flap its wings!

DRAW A BUTTERFLY ON THE UNDERSIDE OF A PAPER PLATE AND COLOR IT WITH PAINT OR MARKERS.

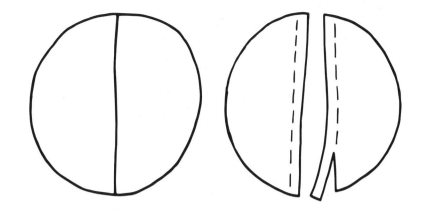

CUT ANOTHER PAPER PLATE IN HALF, AND TRIM 1 INCH OFF OF EACH HALF

FOLD THE BUTTERFLY PLATE IN HALF, PRESSING THE WINGS TOGETHER

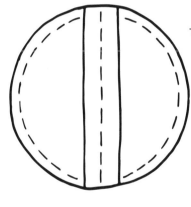

STAPLE THE CUT PLATE PIECES TO THE BACK OF THE BUTTERFLY PLATE, LEAVING THE OPENING ALONG THE FOLD

INSERT YOUR HAND IN THE BACK AND MAKE THE BUTTERFLY'S WINGS MOVE

MATERIALS

2 WHITE PAPER PLATES

COLORED MARKERS OR TEMPERA PAINTS AND BRUSH

SCISSORS

STAPLER

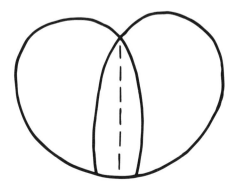

91

DRYING & PRESERVING SPRING FLOWERS

Take a wildflower walk and bring along a thick telephone book or catalog. As you find pretty flowers you want to keep, lay each one gently on a page of the telephone book. (Be sure it is okay to pick them first. Some plants are endangered species or may be on private property.) Arrange the petals and leaves so they lie flat and close the book. Skip about ten pages between flowers. Small blossoms dry best, but so do ferns and pretty leaves.

It takes between a week and a month for the flowers to dry completely. When dried, you can glue them to construction paper or mat board and frame. You can also glue them to paper to create unique greeting cards and stationery. After drying,

some flowers lose their color. You can touch up the petals by delicately painting them with watercolors. Add a few drops of dish detergent to your paint water to help it adhere to the petals.

Another drying method works well if you have a whole bouquet of flowers. Gather the stems together and tie or bind with a rubber band. Then hang the bunch by the stems from a string. They can be tied to a clothesline but should be hung indoors in a shed, garage, or attic and kept out of sunlight and dampness. They should be stiff and dry in about a week and a half. Arrange them in baskets or vases. Weeds, pods, strawflowers, statice, and money plant dry well with this method.

You can also dry flowers by placing them in a borax and sand mixture. To 3 parts of borax, add 1 part heavy, clean, fine sand. Use a large container such as a cardboard box or wastebasket.

Pick the flowers by cutting them with long stems, using a knife or scissors. To cover them with the sand mixture, place some sand in the bottom of the container, and while holding the flower by the stem, gently pour the sand mixture around it until the blossom is submerged. It takes about three weeks for the blossom to dry. When dry, gently sift away the sand and remove the flower.

When you have enough flowers dried to make a bouquet, place the blossoms on stem wires by laying the wire next to the stem of the blossom. Wrap with green floral tape to secure the stem to the stem wire. When finished, you can spray the flowers with an acrylic spray finish if you want. This protects them against humidity.

LET THE FLOWERS HANG UPSIDE DOWN TO DRY

PAPEL PICADO

"Papel picado" means "pierced paper" in Spanish and is created by skilled artists using layers of tissue paper and sharp instruments like nails to punch designs. The paper is used to decorate homes and shops in Mexico.

To create some for your own home, use brightly colored tissue paper. Cut a sheet into smaller sections and fold the sheet, smaller and smaller. Using sharp scissors, cut out designs along the folded edges. Cut small, geometric shapes. When the paper is unfolded, the cut designs will appear in interesting patterns.

To hang your papel picado, fold the top edge over a long piece of string. Fold the paper over about 1/2 inch and tape it securely. Add more pieces until your string is full and tack it up across your room.

CINCO DE MAYO
PROJECTS

MATERIALS

COLORED TISSUE PAPER

SCISSORS

STRING OR YARN

TAPE

MAY 5 IS A BIG HOLIDAY IN MEXICO. ON MAY 5, 1862, MEXICAN FORCES WITHSTOOD FRENCH FORCES WHO WERE TRYING TO TAKE OVER MEXICO FOR NAPOLEON. YOU CAN CREATE PAPEL PICADO AND SOME PAPER BAG PIÑATAS TO HAVE A PARTY OF YOUR OWN.

PAPER BAG PIÑATA

Cut the tissue into strips about 3 inches wide. Cut the strips into fringe, leaving about 1 inch uncut at the top edge. Starting at the bottom of the paper bag, glue the strips around the bag. Glue the next strip so that the fringe comes down and covers the glued area of the first strip. Layer the strips of fringe until the bag is covered. Cut several long streamers of various colors and glue them to the sides and bottom so they will hang and flutter.

With the hole punch, punch holes around the top of the bag, about 2 inches apart. Thread the yarn or string through the holes.

Fill the bag with candies or prizes. Pull the strings up securely and knot. Use the long string ends to tie your piñata where it can be hit with sticks. To break the pinata, Mexican children use sticks. Since your pinata will not be as hard to break as the ones you can buy in Mexico, you can make your own stick. Roll up a newspaper, taping securely with masking tape. Now you are ready for the blindfold!

Swat at the pinata and let your friends gather the goodies as they fall!

MATERIALS

SCISSORS

SEVERAL PIECES OF BRIGHTLY COLORED TISSUE PAPER

BROWN PAPER BAG, LUNCH-SIZE OR LARGER

GLUE

STRING OR YARN

HOLE PUNCH

YARN

CANDIES OR PRIZES

NEWSPAPER

TAPE

3 INCHES

CUT THE TISSUE PAPER STRIPS INTO FRINGE

GLUE STRIPS TO THE BAG STARTING AT THE BOTTOM

FILL WITH GOODIES, TIE SHUT WITH THE YARN, HANG UP, AND START SWINGING

SUMMER FUN

CLIP BOARD

Cut a piece of adhesive paper large enough to cover the cardboard with extra on all edges for overlapping. The paper should be at least 20 inches wide and 14 inches long. Peel off the paper backing and lay the paper on the table with the sticky side up.

Place the cardboard in the center of the adhesive paper, fold the ends toward the center, and then overlap and smooth down the edges. Use the clothespins to hold down your drawing paper during outdoor sketching. If you want to use your clipboard for writing stories or letters, use a metal spring clip to hold the paper at the top of the clipboard. With the hole punch, punch a hole in the clipboard. Tie one end of the yarn piece through the hole. Tie the other end to your pencil.

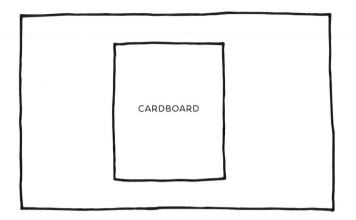

CARDBOARD

LAY CARDBOARD IN CENTER
OF ADHESIVE-BACKED PAPER
(STICKY SIDE UP)

USE SPRING-TYPE CLOTHESPINS TO
SECURE THE PAPER TO THE CLIPBOARD
FOR OUTDOOR SKETCHING

PUNCH A HOLE AND TIE
ON A PENCIL WITH A
LENGTH OF YARN

MATERIALS

VINYL ADHESIVE-BACKED PAPER

1 (9 X 12-INCH) PIECE OF HEAVY CARDBOARD
(GROCERY BOXES ARE PERFECT)

4 SPRING-TYPE WOODEN CLOTHESPINS

YARN: 1 (30-INCH) PIECE

SCISSORS

HOLE PUNCH

PENCIL

HULA SKIRT

Warm summer days are the time for a little hula dancing. Create your own Hawaiian costume. Hula skirts are quick, cheap, and fun and can be tied on over your regular clothing.

You'll need to work on the floor for this one. Pile up some paper to work from. Cut a strip of tape about 6 inches longer than your waist measurement. Lay the tape on the floor, sticky side up. Make the skirt by laying one end of the paper strips on top of the tape. Place the strips next to each other—the closer together, the more skirt to sway.

When the length of tape is full of paper strips, lay another piece of tape on top of the first one and press together to create a waistband. Wrap the skirt around your waist. Overlap and fasten with a large safety pin or more masking tape.

Every hula skirt needs a few leis to complete the outfit. Make a flower template out of cardboard or tagboard. Trace and cut out tissue paper flowers. Cutting through three layers of tissue at once goes faster. Punch a hole in the center of each flower.

Cut the straws into 1-inch-long pieces. Cut a piece of string or yarn about 30 inches long.

String a straw piece first and knot the yarn around it so the pieces won't fall off as you continue stringing.

String the straw pieces, putting three paper flowers between each section of straw. Knot the ends to create a long necklace.

FLOWER LEIS

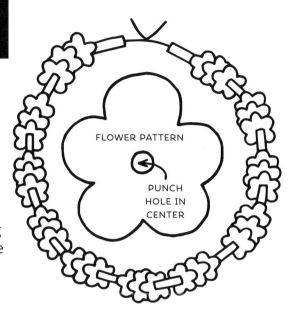

FLOWER PATTERN

PUNCH HOLE IN CENTER

STRAW PIECES WITH STRING

MATERIALS

NEWSPRINT OR BUTCHER PAPER CUT INTO LONG STRIPS (PIECES SHOULD BE ABOUT 1/4 INCH WIDE AND ABOUT 2 FEET LONG)

SCISSORS

1-INCH-WIDE MASKING TAPE

MATERIALS

CARDBOARD OR TAGBOARD: 1 (5 X 5-INCH) PIECE

PENCIL

SCISSORS

COLORED TISSUE PAPER, SMALL PIECES IN SEVERAL COLORS

HOLE PUNCH

DRINKING STRAWS, 6 FOR EACH LEI

STRING OR YARN, ABOUT 30 INCHES LONG

97

RIBBON STICKS

Cut 3 (36-inch-long) paper streamers. You can use all one color or a variety. Holding the three ends together, wrap the crepe papers around the end of the straw, tucking the cut edges under. Staple to the straw.

MATERIALS

SCISSORS

CREPE PAPER STREAMERS

DRINKING STRAWS

STAPLER

STAPLE PAPER STREAMERS TO A STRAW

PAPER PLEASERS

FOLD SO A MEETS B

FOLD SO C MEETS D AND E MEETS F

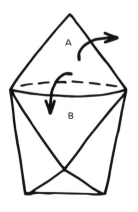

FOLD A AND B DOWN.

PAPER CUPS

Fold the paper so A and B meet.

Then, fold so C meets D.

Fold E up to meet F.

A and B are now the tips. Fold them down on each side.

You can fill with water and drink up!

MATERIALS

1 (8 X 8–INCH) PIECE OF PAPER

FILL WITH WATER!

STARFISH

Cut the poster board and construction paper into identical star shapes. Glue together. Spread glue all over the yellow star. Sprinkle the cornmeal into the wet glue and then shake off the excess cornmeal when the glue has dried. Make several starfish in a variety of sizes.

MATERIALS

SCISSORS

POSTERBOARD

YELLOW CONSTRUCTION PAPER

WHITE GLUE

CORNMEAL

A DAY AT THE BEACH

SUMMER DAYS MAKE YOU THINK OF THE BEACH. WITH A FEW ODDS AND ENDS YOU CAN TAKE YOURSELF AWAY ON A BEACH VACATION, RIGHT AT HOME!

CUT 1 FROM POSTERBOARD AND 1 FROM YELLOW PAPER

SAILBOAT

Experiment a little to find out how much sand you need to put into your bottle to keep the boat floating upright. If it tilts in the water, try adding a little more sand. Once upright, screw the lid on firmly.

Cut out boat and sail shapes from the construction paper and add details with markers. Staple the pieces around the bottles and tape securely. Make several boats or a flotilla and fill up the backyard wading pool. You might want to add a *Mayflower*, *Noah's Ark*, the *Jolly Roger* . . . or maybe even the *Titanic*!

MATERIALS

PLASTIC SODA BOTTLE

SAND OR SOIL

SCISSORS

COLORED CONSTRUCTION PAPER

MARKERS

STAPLER

TAPE

SUN VISORS

Use the pattern to trace and cut out a visor from the poster board. Decorate with brightly colored markers.

Cut a piece of elastic about 10 inches long. Staple one end to the visor. Adjust it to fit your head snugly. Staple the other end to the visor. Trim away the extra elastic.

MATERIALS

PENCIL

COLORED POSTER BOARD

COLORED MARKERS

SCISSORS

ELASTIC BRAID, 1/4 INCH WIDE

STAPLER

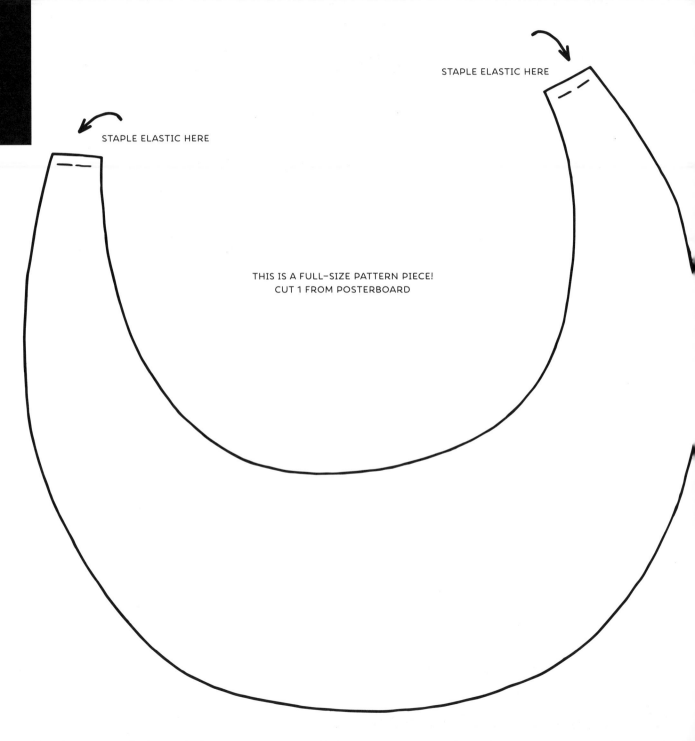

STAPLE ELASTIC HERE

STAPLE ELASTIC HERE

THIS IS A FULL-SIZE PATTERN PIECE!
CUT 1 FROM POSTERBOARD

MINI PALM TREES

Trace and cut out 2 or 3 palm leaves from the green paper. With the marker, draw detail lines on the leaves. Cut a piece of brown paper to cover the tissue tube. Glue it around the tube. Draw a design with the marker to create the look of a palm tree's textured bark. Fold the tab down on the leaves and insert them into the end of the trunk. Pinch the trunk over the tabs and staple everything together. Staple twice to secure it.

MATERIALS

PENCIL

SCISSORS

GREEN & BROWN CONSTRUCTION PAPER

BLACK MARKER

TOILET TISSUE TUBE

STAPLER

STAPLE LEAVES INTO TOP OF THE TUBE

WHAT'S A BEACH WITHOUT PALM TREES? MAKE SOME OF YOUR OWN TO DECORATE YOUR ROOM. IF YOU HAVE SOME CLAY DINOSAURS, THESE PALM TREES HELP THEM FEEL RIGHT AT HOME.

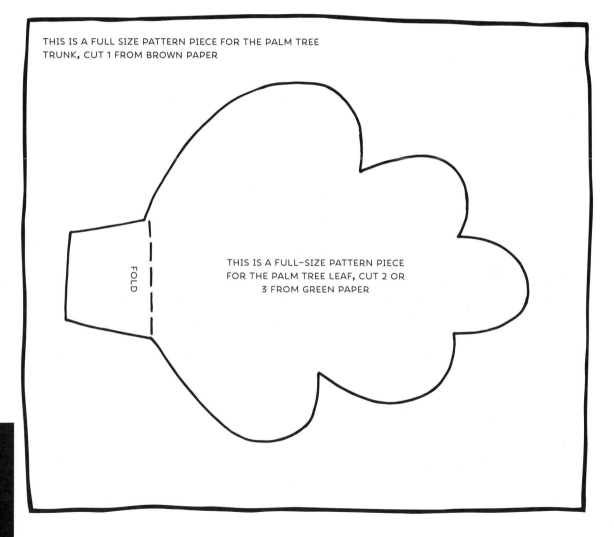

THIS IS A FULL SIZE PATTERN PIECE FOR THE PALM TREE TRUNK, CUT 1 FROM BROWN PAPER

FOLD

THIS IS A FULL-SIZE PATTERN PIECE FOR THE PALM TREE LEAF, CUT 2 OR 3 FROM GREEN PAPER

SAND CANDLES

First, pour about 1/4 cup of salt into each bowl. Squirt a few drops of food coloring into the salt—one color per bowl—and mix it well.

Pour the colored salt into the baby food jar, making each layer of color about 1/4 inch to 1/2 inch deep. Do not shake. Leave the top inch of the jar unfilled.

TOURIST SHOPS AT THE BEACH OFTEN SELL ITEMS MADE BY LAYERING COLORED SAND INTO A CONTAINER. YOU CAN USE SALT INSTEAD OF SAND AND CREATE A CANDLE IN ITS OWN HOLDER. LAYERS OF COLORED SALT CAN BE USED TO FILL JARS OF ALL SHAPES AND SIZES. IF FILLED TO THE VERY TOP, THEY OFTEN HOLD THE LAYERED LOOK FOR A LONG TIME AND MAKE HANDSOME GIFTS.

Melt the wax carefully in a can placed in the top of a double boiler at low heat (both top and bottom of double boiler should have water in them).

Have an adult pour hot wax into the jar over the top of the salt. Fill the jar almost to the top.

While the wax is still hot and has not yet begun to set up, drop the piece of wick into the wax, letting about 1 inch of wick stick out at the top.

Let the candle cool undisturbed.

WARNING: BE CAREFUL; WAX WILL CATCH FIRE IF IT GETS TOO HOT. MAKE SURE AN ADULT HELPS WITH THE WAX PART OF THIS PROJECT.

MATERIALS

SALT: ABOUT 1/3 BOX OR CANISTER FOR EACH CANDLE

SMALL BOWL FOR EACH COLOR OF SALT

FOOD COLORING, VARIOUS COLORS

EMPTY BABY FOOD JAR

PARAFFIN WAX OR CANDLE WAX

EMPTY CAN TO MELT WAX IN

DOUBLE BOILER

CANDLE WICK, ABOUT 2 INCHES LONG

WICK WAS SET DOWN IN THE WAX BEFORE IT COOLED

1 INCH OF WAX TO THE TOP OF THE JAR

LAYERS OF COLORED SALT

PLAY SKATEBOARD OR SCOOTER

MATERIALS

- CRAFT KNIFE
- POPSICLE STICKS OR TONGUE DEPRESSORS
- SAND PAPER
- SCISSORS
- PLASTIC DRINKING STRAWS
- COLORED MARKERS
- GLUE

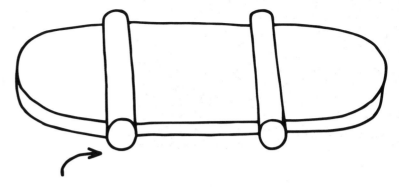

GLUE STRAW PIECES TO THE BOTTOM OF THE BOARD

Cut the Popsicle stick about 2 inches long. Sand the rough edges using sandpaper or by rubbing against a cement sidewalk, rounding the cut edge to match the other end. Cut two sections of straw, both as wide as the Popsicle stick. Color the stick with markers. Glue the straw sections to the bottom of the board to resemble wheels.

If you want to turn your board into a scooter, cut another section of drinking straw about 2 inches long. Cut a shorter piece about 1 inch long. Glue the 2 to create a T-shape for the scooter handlebar. When dry, glue the handlebar section to the top of the board section. Hold in position until the glue dries.

GLUE PIECES IN PLACE TO CREATE A SCOOTER

SKATEBOARD RAMP

Using the diagrams, measure and cut out two sides from the foam core board. Make them identical. Then cut out the two tops from foam core as well. Cut the rectangle from mat board or heavy poster board.

Curve and tape the rectangle to the curved sections, holding the board in place as you tape. Do one side, then form and tape the other. Tape the strips into place at the top to create platforms.

MATERIALS

PENCIL

CRAFT KNIFE

FOAM CORE BOARD

MAT BOARD

MASKING TAPE

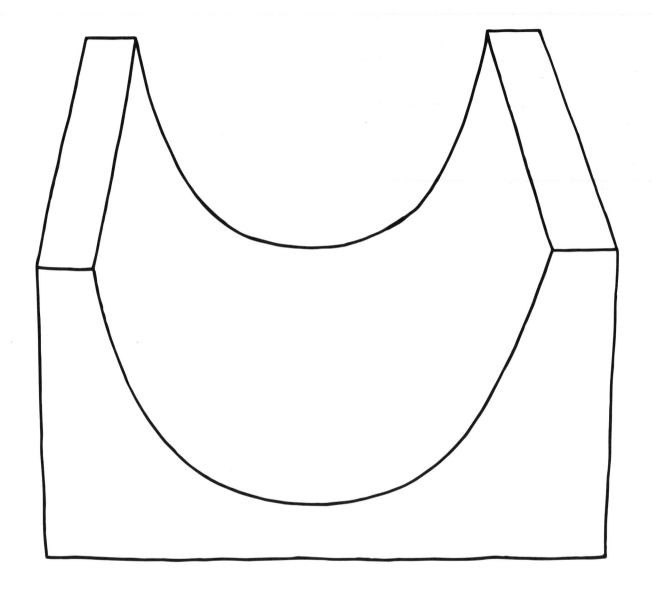

CREATE A RAMP FOR YOUR SKATEBOARDS
TO DO TRICKS AND STUNTS

TAPE THE PIECES TOGETHER

SIDE

TOP RAIL

CUT 2 TOPS LIKE THIS

CUT A RECTANGLE
THAT'S 6 3/4 X 11
INCHES FOR THE
INSIDE PART

CUT 2 SIDES LIKE THIS

BALLOON SCULPTURES

Amaze and entertain your friends with the things you can make from balloons.

Clowning around with balloons is easy to do. The secret is in using balloons made especially for balloon sculpture. Look in your local phone directory for shops that carry party or magic supplies. The size professional clowns recommend is called #245 or #260-A of the A series. These balloons are long and pencil shaped.

To sculpt, follow the diagrams. Inflate the balloon, leaving a portion uninflated. This allows the air in the balloon to expand as you create twists. Knot the end of the balloon.

Balloon shapes are created by forming bubbles in the balloon. The bubbles are held in place by a lock twist to prevent the balloon from untwisting. A basic lock twist is made by pinching the air out of a small area. Twist the two sections in opposite directions until they don't unwind when you let go.

*See warning, page 69.

MOUSE

Inflate the balloon until the balloon is about 12 inches long. The uninflated section will be the tail. Knot the end.

Twist 1 (2-inch) bubble and 2 (1-inch) bubbles.

Lock twist the 2 (1-inch) bubbles at the base to form the ears.

MATERIALS

BALLOONS, #245 OR #260-A*

WATERCOLOR MARKERS

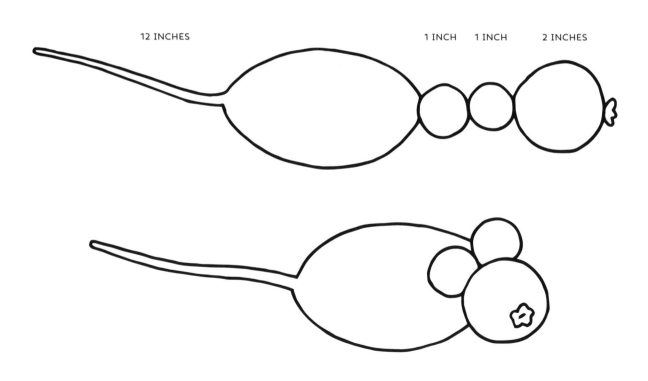

12 INCHES   1 INCH   1 INCH   2 INCHES

SWAN

Inflate a balloon, leaving about 2 inches uninflated. Knot the end. Pinch off a 4-inch section next to the uninflated end. Twist this area with a bubble about 1 inch from the knotted end until the 2 sections are locked.

Use a watercolor marker to gently dot on an eye.

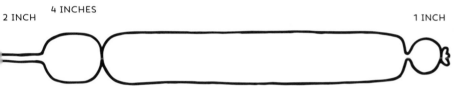

2 INCH   4 INCHES   1 INCH

TWIST TOGETHER
BETWEEN THE
TWO BUBBLES

USE WATERCOLOR MARKERS
TO DRAW ON AN EYE

APPLE

To make an apple, you need to use a short balloon with a colored tip. A red balloon with a green tip looks best. These can be purchased at party and clown supply shops.
Blow the balloon up, leaving 1 inch empty at the tip. Knot the end. Push the knot into the middle of the balloon until your fingers can pinch hold of it through the tip of the balloon. Pull the knot up and twist firmly. The twist around the knot becomes the stem.

GREEN TIP   RED

USE A SPECIAL "APPLE" BALLOON

BLOW IT UP, LEAVING THE
TIP EMPTY

PUSH THE KNOT THROUGH &
PULL IT UP THROUGH THE TIP

TWIST TIP AROUND
THE KNOT TO MAKE
A STEM

CRYSTAL GARDEN

An old-fashioned project that always provides wonder and excitement is the crystal garden. Gather several small stones or use barbecue briquettes. Either will work just fine. The bluing may be difficult to find. Look in the laundry supply section of grocery stores. It's in a small blue bottle, usually next to the starch and bleach products.

Place the briquettes or stones in the bowl. Mix all the other ingredients together, except the food coloring. Pour the mixture over the stones with a spoon. You may have extra; just store it in a covered container and add to the garden over the next few days to keep it growing.

Drop food coloring over the coated stones.

Crystals will begin to form in about twenty minutes. Pour more solution and add more coloring every day, and the garden will continue to change and grow.

MATERIALS

6 TO 7 CHARCOAL BRIQUETTES OR STONES

SHALLOW BOWL

6 TABLESPOONS SALT

6 TABLESPOONS LAUNDRY BLUING

6 TABLESPOONS WATER

1 TABLESPOON AMMONIA

FOOD COLORING

PUT STONES OR CHARCOAL BRIQUETTES IN A SHALLOW BOWL

ADD THE MIXTURE AND FOOD COLORING

THE GARDEN WILL MYSTERIOUSLY GROW

WALKING SNAKE

MATERIALS

SCISSORS

FOAM RUBBER STRIP: 2 X 36 INCHES

RUBBER BAND

COPPER WIRE

MARKERS

SMALL PIECE OF RED FELT

GLUE

You can make your own clever walking snakes that are sold at fairs and carnivals. As you walk, hold the wire in your hand and guide the snake along the ground. The wire will not be very visible, so the snake appears to walk alone.

With scissors, trim the foam strip so it tapers to a point at one end. This will be the tail end.

Wrap the rubber band tightly around the other end, about 3 inches from the end. This will create a neck. Slip one end of the wire under the rubber band and twist it together firmly. With the snake on the floor and the wire in your hand, trim the wire, leaving 3 inches extra. Roll these 3 inches back and wrap it around itself to create a handle.

Decorate the snake with the markers, create a tongue out of felt, and glue it to the head. Draw on some eyes, and he's ready for a walk.

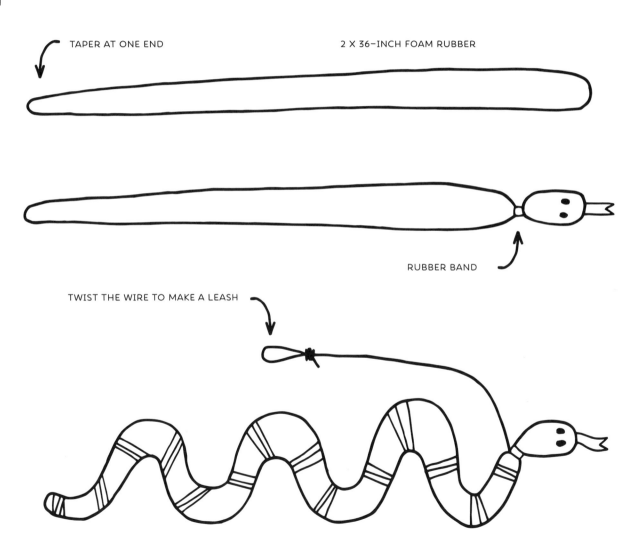

TAPER AT ONE END

2 X 36-INCH FOAM RUBBER

RUBBER BAND

TWIST THE WIRE TO MAKE A LEASH

WALKING INVISIBLE DOG

shape the wire so it curves down a bit. Now when you walk your invisible dog, hold the wire in front of you as you walk so the dog appears to be wearing the collar.

The best thing about the invisible dog is that she only needs to go out when you want to!

MATERIALS

SMALL DOG COLLAR

WHITE GLUE

STURDY WIRE

Another popular carnival toy is the invisible dog. All you need is a small dog collar and sturdy wire. If you have a leash, that's even better.

Soak the collar in white glue, shaping it while it's still wet so it will be round. Allow to dry. If you have a leather collar, it may not need stiffening.

Cut your wire so it will extend from your hand to about 5 inches from the floor. Add 3 inches for twisting the ends under.

If you are using a leash, insert the wire through the chains.

Fasten the wire to the collar by twisting it around the top and tucking the cut ends under so they can't be seen. Twist the other end of the wire and tuck the sharp edge inside so you won't cut your hand. Gently

DOGGIE BANK

Position the milk jugs as shown. With the hot glue gun, glue the jugs together securely to create a head and body.

Use the glue gun to glue the eyes on both sides of the head.

Trim the 6 x 8-inch felt pieces so they are rounded on the corners and slightly smaller at one end. These are the dog's ears. Position them at the sides of the head, with the smaller end at the top. Use the glue gun to dot a line of glue across the top end of the ear. Press it into place on the dog's head.

The 2 x 12-inch felt strip is a collar for the dog and hides the glued neck area. Position it around the dog's neck, trim it to fit, and secure in place with the glue gun.

Use the black marker to color the jug's snap-on lid completely black. It is the nose. Snap it back on the jug. With the marker, draw a mouth on the front and side area of the dog's face.

Position and glue the long felt strip in place on the body, creating the dog's tail.

With a craft knife, slice a slit somewhere on the dog's back so you can insert coins. Ask an adult to help with this because these jugs are slippery.

When you are ready to take money out of the bank, remove the lid from the back end of the dog and shake it out.

MATERIALS

2 (1-GALLON) MILK JUGS WITH SNAP-ON LIDS

HOT GLUE GUN

SCISSORS

2 (1-INCH) DECORATIVE EYES (OPTIONAL)

2 (6 X 8-INCH) BLACK PIECES OF FELT FOR THE EARS

1 (2 X 12-INCH) BROWN FELT STRIP FOR THE DOG'S COLLAR

BLACK PERMANENT MARKER

1 (1 X 12-INCH) BLACK FELT STRIP FOR THE TAIL

CRAFT KNIFE

BLACK NOSE

BLACK FELT EARS

BLACK FELT TAIL

BROWN FELT COLLAR

SLIT FOR MONEY

SPARKLE PAINTS

Mix equal parts of flour, water, and salt. Pour some of the mixture in each squeeze bottle. Add tempera paint to each bottle and shake well.

Squeeze the paint onto paper, creating a design, word, or picture.

Let dry. When the paint is dry, the salt makes the picture sparkle.

If you like, you can brush the paints on instead of squeezing them.

MATERIALS

FLOUR

WATER

SALT

EMPTY SQUEEZABLE BOTTLES

TEMPERA PAINT

PAPER

BUBBLE FUN

Mix up the dish soap, some water, and a spoonful of glycerin in a pan. You don't absolutely need the glycerin, but it makes the bubbles last longer and get larger without breaking.

Create your own wand, bending the wire into whatever shape you wish.

Dip the wand in the soap solution and wave in the air to create zillions of super bubbles.

MATERIALS

LIQUID DISH SOAP
(JOY WORKS BEST)

WATER

GLYCERIN (AVAILABLE AT DRUG STORES)

FLAT CAKE OR PIE TINS, LARGER TINS FOR LARGE WANDS

THIN WIRE

HEAVY-DUTY SCISSORS TO CUT THE WIRE

PRETTY BUBBLES

SUMMER IS FOR BLOWING GIANT SOAP BUBBLES. YOU CAN MAKE YOUR OWN BUBBLE SOLUTION AND CREATE HUGE BUBBLES.

Want to create really huge ones? Of course you do! Use 2 drinking straws and a length of string, about 48 inches long. Thread the string through both of the straws and knot the ends. Lay the straws and string down in the soap solution. Gently lift up the straws, one in each hand. Spread the straws apart as you lift, and a giant bubble will form. Wave your arms through the air, and it will be set free to float up, up, and away!

TWIST WIRE INTO FUN SHAPES FOR MAKING BUBBLES

TO MAKE A GIANT SOAP BUBBLE WAND, TIE 48 INCHES OF STRING BETWEEN 2 PLASTIC STRAWS

BUBBLE ART NOTEPAPER

Cut the printer paper in half or fourths. Mix the soap and water in equal amounts. Add one color of tempera to each of the cups. Use the straw to blow air into the paint mixture until it bubbles and froths up. While the bubbles are still full, gently lay the paper surface over the bubbles. They will stick to the paper, then collapse. They will leave their colorful print on the paper.

Let dry. Then fold paper in half to create cards, stationery, or gift wrap.

MATERIALS

SCISSORS

PRINTER PAPER

DISH SOAP

WATER

TEMPERA PAINTS

TEA CUPS OR PAPER CUPS

DRINKING STRAWS

MARBLEIZING IS A GREAT WAY TO CREATE SPECIAL STATIONERY, AND WHEN YOU DIP AN ORDINARY PENCIL INTO THE MIXTURE, IT WILL COME OUT TO MATCH. MARBLEIZING CREATES A REALLY BEAUTIFUL PATTERN. THE SECRET IS IN CHOOSING COLORS THAT LOOK NICE TOGETHER. YOU CAN USE SPRAY PAINT IN THE PROJECT, SO IT'S A GOOD WAY TO USE UP ALL THOSE ODDS AND ENDS OF SPRAY PAINT IN THE GARAGE. OR YOU CAN USE OIL–BASED HOUSE PAINT OR ARTIST'S OIL TUBE COLORS.

MARBLES PAPER & PENCILS

MATERIALS

NEWSPAPERS SPREAD OUT FOR A PROJECT DRYING AREA

BUCKET OF WATER

OIL–BASED PAINTS

WOODEN PAINT STIRRER OR STICK

PENCILS FOR DIPPING

PRINTER OR CONSTRUCTION PAPER

Work outdoors or in a well-ventilated area. Cover everything around you with the newspapers because this project can be messy. Oil paints do not wash off with water.

Fill bucket with water to about 2 inches from the top. If you are using spray paints, spray some paint onto the water for about 4–5 seconds. Add another color, overlapping the colors. If you use liquid oil paints, spoon or pour a few tablespoonfuls onto the water. If you are using oil tube paints, mix the paint to

SWIRL PAINT AROUND ON TOP OF THE WATER. LAY PAPER DOWN ON THE PAINT AND IT WILL STICK TO THE PAPER

HANG PAPER TO DRY

DIP PENCILS IN THE PAINT AND STICK THEM IN AN EGG CARTON TO DRY

a creamy consistency with some turpentine then drop by spoonfuls onto the water. Use the stick to spread the paint around on the top of the water and create interesting swirls, being careful not to mix the colors completely together.

Lay a piece of paper on the surface of the water. It will pick up the paint in its swirled design. When dipping pencils, hold by the eraser and roll the pencil over the surface of the water, picking up the paint as you roll.

Lay the paper on the newspapers or hang with clips and let dry. To let pencils dry, stick them into the bottom of empty egg cartons. It takes several hours to dry.

If you like, you can purchase a disposable aluminum roasting pan at the grocery store and use it instead of the bucket. That way, you won't have to clean the oil paints out of the bucket when you are through. Just throw the roasting pan away or keep for another project.

STAINED GLASS LEAF PICTURES

MATERIALS

COLORFUL FALL LEAVES

WAX PAPER

OLD NEWSPAPER

STEAM IRON

SCISSORS

GLUE OR PASTE

CONSTRUCTION PAPER STRIPS: 1 INCH WIDE

Place a few leaves in an interesting arrangement between 2 pieces of wax paper. Lay a piece of newspaper over the wax paper. Press gently with a warm steam iron. The wax paper melts together, sealing around the leaf. Trim the wax paper edges with scissors and glue the construction paper strips over the edges, creating a frame.

These "stained glass" pieces look nice taped on windows so sunlight can shine through.

NEWSPAPER

WAX PAPER

LEAVES

GLUE PAPER STRIPS TO CREATE A FRAME

SEED MOSAICS

It's easier to work with a wide variety of seeds and pods if you sort each seed type into its own paper cup or small bowl. Then take out only what you need so they won't get all mixed up. Start by spreading glue on a small area of the cardboard. Then set seeds into the glue in your own arrangement. You might want to create interesting patterns of shapes and colors or create a scene using the natural color and texture of the seeds to express your ideas.

GLUE

INDIAN CORN COLLAGE

Draw an outline of a corncob if you choose, or do the printing freehand. Print kernels of corn by dipping your finger into the paint and pressing onto the paper. Keep changing colors without washing your finger, because Indian corn has blended colors. Press the paint spots in the shape of an ear of corn. When the paint dries, glue corn husks down so it looks more like a real ear of Indian corn. If you can't find corn husks, cut out and glue on husks made from crepe paper or construction paper.

MATERIALS

ASSORTED TINY SEEDS: CORN, BEAN, SUNFLOWER, FENNEL, DILL, WATERMELON, SQUASH, LENTILS, PEARL BARLEY, KIDNEY BEANS; ALSO SEED PODS FROM WEEDS, TREES, AND BUSHES

PAPER CUPS OR SMALL BOWLS

PIECE OF CARDBOARD

WHITE GLUE

MATERIALS

CONSTRUCTION PAPER

TEMPERA PAINT: ORANGE, YELLOW, AND BLUE

DRIED CORN HUSKS (FROM LOCAL GARDENERS OR FARMERS, ROADSIDE STANDS, CRAFT STORE, OR MEXICAN FOOD SECTION OF GROCERY STORE)

GLUE

OLD-FASHIONED CRAFTS

APPLE PEOPLE

Apples were a popular material that pioneers used to create dolls or interesting characters.

Use any kind of apple. Peel it carefully, keeping the surface as smooth as you can. Use a knife or spoon to carve the features. Because the apple will shrink and wrinkle up as it dries, the face will look different from the one you cut into the fresh apple. You may want to carve several apples and pick out your favorite one later when they are all dry. Make a few cuts across the apple forehead to give wrinkled lines there.

When you have carved out a simple nose, a mouth, and eye sockets, paint the head with a mixture of lemon juice and salt to bleach the skin color.

You can attach a string to the stem to hang it or push a wire or Popsicle stick into the apple and let it stand in a short jar. Put in a warm place for three weeks.

When the head is dry, paint it with tempera or watercolors if you want, rouge the cheeks with a little powder blush makeup, or leave in its natural state.

You will have to stick something dark and round into the eye sockets for eyes. Use whole cloves, nails, beads, seeds, or bead-topped straight pins.

MATERIALS

APPLE, PEELED

KNIFE OR SPOON

LEMON JUICE & SALT MIXTURE

STRING, POPSICLE STICK, OR WIRE

JAR

TEMPERA OR WATERCOLOR PAINTS

CLOVES, BEADS, SEEDS, CORN FOR EYES AND TEETH

PIPE CLEANERS OR WIRE

LONG-NECKED BOTTLE

GLUE

CLOTH

CARVE THE FEATURES

LET THE APPLE DRY

The mouth can show a row of teeth made by using seeds, corn, rice, or tiny pearls, sticking or gluing them in place inside the mouth opening.

To make hands and feet, use apple slices and carve them a little. Let dry just like the head. You can also use pieces of felt for the hands.

For arms and legs, use pipe cleaners, wire, or strips of twisted paper to make clothes.

The body can be made from a long-necked bottle. When the head dries, glue it to the bottle. Then drape cloth over the bottle body to make clothes.

You can also use wire for the body, shaping it like the drawing. Wrap strips of soft cloth over the wire to build up a body. Cut and glue cloth onto the body to create the clothing. Create a stand for your figure from a block of wood.

A WIRE BODY CAN BE BENT INTO A SHAPE

CORN HUSK DOLLS

Dolls made from the husks of corn were made by pioneer and Native American children. Make your own with husks from your garden, a craft shop, or grocery store (check the Mexican food section). Soak the dry husks in water for five minutes. Tear some of the husks into long strips to be used later for tying bundles together.

Roll strips of husk into a ball and wrap in a rectangular piece of husk. Tie at the bottom for a neck.

Draw a face on it with a colored marker. Use corn silk or yarn for hair. Glue it to the doll's head.

Arms can be made two ways:

1. Tightly roll a few long pieces of husk and tie with husk strips about 1/2 inch from each end to make a wrist and hand. Tie tightly again in the middle.

2. Cover a pipe cleaner by rolling a strip of husk around it. Then cover with a sheet of husk and tie the same as above.

After you have a finished arm section, tie it to the backbone at the neck level. Attach the arms to the head as in the drawing, binding the sections together with strips of husk.

A body is made by rolling 15 to 20 husks together and tying at the waist. The lower half should be slightly longer to look like a skirt.

Insert the head and arm section into the body and tie at the neck.

To make a boy doll, make the legs the same way as the arms and tie to the chest with strips of husk.

MATERIALS

CORN HUSKS

WATER

COLORED MARKER

CORN SILK OR YARN

GLUE

ROLL AND TIE HUSKS OR ROLL A HUSK AROUND A PIPECLEANER AND TIE

MAKE A HEAD AND DRAW A FACE WITH MARKER

TIE ARMS TO HEAD BELOW THE NECK

TIE BODY HUSKS TOGETHER AT WAIST

TIE BODY TO CHEST SECTION AT THE NECK AND FOLD THE HUSKS DOWN TO MAKE A COLLAR

BRAIDED RUG

You can make a real braided rug for your room. Use fabric pieces or old clothes torn into strips.

Cut or tear the fabric into strips that are 1 inch to 2 inches wide.

Sew 3 strips together at one end. Braid the them together. They don't have to be the same length, because as you get to the end of a strip, sew another one to it with needle and thread and keep on going.

When your braided piece gets to be about 3 feet long, start coiling it into a rug. Twist the braided strip around the end you started with, keeping it flat as you go, wrapping it around and around. Sometimes it's easier to start by twisting the beginning around a small piece of cardboard or a wad of paper. Sew the coil in place as you go with a heavy needle and strong thread. Continue wrapping and sewing until the rug is as big as you want.

When the rug is just as you want it, tuck the loose ends of fabric back into the braid and stitch the ending in place with needle and thread. Small rugs can be used as coasters, covers for wooden seats, or whatever you choose.

MATERIALS

SCISSORS

FABRIC PIECES TORN INTO STRIPS

NEEDLE & THREAD

BRAID THE STRIPS TOGETHER

SEW THE COIL IN PLACE TO CREATE A RUG

OAT BOX CRADLE

Make a cradle that really rocks for your doll. You will need an oatmeal container, the kind that is shaped like a large tube. Cut it into a cradle shape, just like the drawing.

You can paint the cradle, but covering it with wallpaper scraps or fabric pieces is also fun. Use scissors to trim the fabric or paper to fit. Glue it in place. Add a little lace trim or any decoration you like around the edges if you want.

Extra fabric can be cut to line the inside of the cradle, too. If you have enough, cut some to make a matching blanket to keep the doll or teddy bear cozy.

MATERIALS

OATMEAL CONTAINER
(CYLINDRICAL SHAPE)

SCISSORS

PAINT, WALLPAPER, OR FABRIC
SCRAPS

GLUE

CUT THE OATMEAL CONTAINER IN A CRADLE SHAPE

COVER WITH PAPER OR FABRIC

JACOB'S LADDER

Sand the wood pieces smooth. Attach the blocks to each other with the twill tape. Cut 2 pieces of twill tape 28 1/2 inches long. Staple or glue the ends of the tape pieces to the edge of the first block. Space the 2 tape pieces 1 1/2 inches apart.

Weave the tapes in and out between the blocks and then staple the ends to the bottom edge of the seventh block.

Weave a third piece of tape (21 1/2 inches long) in and out of the blocks in the opposite direction. Staple or glue the ends to the inside edges of the first block and the last block.

To make Jacob's Ladder work, hold the second block and let the top block tumble down, causing each block below to drop and tumble.

MATERIALS

SANDPAPER

7 (2 1/2 X 3 1/2–INCH) PIECES OF THIN WOOD

TWILL TAPE (FOUND IN FABRIC DEPARTMENTS)

STAPLER OR GLUE GUN

WIND THE TAPE THROUGH THE BLOCKS AS SHOWN. STAPLE TO THE ENDS OF THE BLOCKS

THESE CLATTER BLOCKS HAVE BEEN MADE FOR YEARS. THEY ARE HARD TO FIGURE OUT, BUT IF YOU MAKE THEM, YOU'LL SEE THE SECRET TRICK.

BEAN GHOSTS

Use construction paper to create a ghostly scene: a haunted house with black paper, a spooky graveyard scene, or an old gnarled tree. Glue lima beans in place on the scene, and then add eyes and rounded "O" mouths. The beans are the ghosts in your scary scene.

MATERIALS

CONSTRUCTION PAPER

GLUE

WHITE LIMA BEANS

BLACK PERMANENT FINE–TIP MARKER

SCARY GHOSTS

TISSUE GHOSTS

This ghost project is one everyone tries sooner or later. Use white tissues and a rubber band. Wad up a tissue into a round ball, and then lay it in the center of another tissue. Wrap the second tissue down around the tissue ball and secure it with the rubber band. Use a marker to dot on eyes, and you have a finished ghost!

MATERIALS

TISSUES

RUBBER BAND

MARKER

SPIDERS

Use black pompoms and black pipe cleaners to create spiders to perch everywhere.

Use four pipe cleaners. Tie them all together in the center, using half of another pipe cleaner twisted around them to hold them together. Spread the pipe cleaners apart a little, and fold the ends to create spider legs. Glue a pompom onto the center of the leg section. You can use a paper punch to punch out two red eyes, and then glue them to the pompom.

If you want to create a web for your spider, string some black yarn across a doorway, back and forth, tying the pieces together here and there, using tape to fasten the pieces to the doorway.

MATERIALS

BLACK POMPOMS (1 FOR EACH SPIDER)

BLACK PIPE CLEANERS

HOLE PUNCH

RED FELT

GLUE

SPOOKY SPIDERS

SPIDER WEBS

Cut a piece of black paper to fit in the bottom of the cake pan. Place half a spoonful of white paint in the middle of the paper. Drop a marble into the pan and tilt it back and forth so the marble runs through the paint and leaves a trail of paint that looks like a spider web.

MATERIALS

BLACK CONSTRUCTION PAPER

CAKE PAN

WHITE TEMPERA PAINT

MARBLE

125

PAPER SACK PUMPKINS

To make a paper bag pumpkin, stuff a paper sack with old crumpled newspapers. Gather the open top and crimp edges together. Close the sack with a rubber band to form a stem handle. Paint the sack orange and the stem green. When the paint dries, turn the pumpkins into jack-o'-lanterns by using black paint, markers, or by cutting out paper shapes and pasting on pumpkin for eyes and mouth.

Make a lot of these pumpkins and put them together to make a pumpkin patch. Use green crepe paper streamers to twist vines from the stem of each pumpkin. Group the pumpkins close together and twist leaves and tendrils from the crepe paper.

MATERIALS

BROWN PAPER LUNCH SACKS

OLD NEWSPAPERS

RUBBER BAND

PAINTBRUSH

ORANGE & GREEN TEMPERA PAINT

BLACK PAINT, MARKERS , OR PAPER

GREEN CREPE PAPER

HALLOWEEN DECORATIONS

THESE ARE QUICK AND FUN TO MAKE.

TWIST GREEN CREPE PAPER TO COVER THE STEM AND CREATE LEAVES AND VINES

PAINT THE STUFFED SACK ORANGE

DRAPE THE CLOTH OVER THE ORANGE AND USE PENCILS TO SHAPE ARMS

LET DRY AND GLUE EYES ON

GAUZY GHOSTS

Pour a cup of liquid starch into a small bowl. Dip the cheesecloth in the starch until it's all wet. Set the orange on the top of a drinking glass. Gently drape the wet cheesecloth over the orange, bringing the edges down evenly all around. Use the two pencils to create arms for the ghost. While the starch is still wet, stick the pencils up and drape the fabric gently over them. Use tape to secure the pencils to the sides of the drinking glass, or to the table top.

Let the ghost dry. Glue on eyes.

MATERIALS

LIQUID STARCH

SMALL BOWL

1 (24 X 24-INCH) SQUARE OF CHEESECLOTH

ORANGE OR RUBBER BALL

DRINKING GLASSES

TWO PENCILS

TAPE

GLUE-ON CRAFT EYES OR MAKE EYES FROM WHITE & BLACK FELT PIECES

WITCH PUPPET

MATERIALS

SCISSORS

CARDBOARD EGG CARTON

PENCIL

BLACK CONSTRUCTION PAPER

GLUE

RUG YARN FOR HAIR

BROWN PAPER LUNCH SACK

TWO OR THREE GREEN SPLIT PEAS OR LENTILS

With scissors, cut away the egg carton so that you have a section with 2 egg cups and the protruding divider section that goes between 4 egg cups.

Draw and cut out hat and dress shapes from the black paper.

Cut 2 small black circles for eyes and glue them in the bottom of the egg cup sections.

Cut the yarn into several 6-inch sections and glue to the bag for hair. Glue the hat on top of the yarn.

Glue the dress to the bag. Glue the egg carton section to the bag. It will be the eyes and nose. Draw a wicked mouth on the bag.

Last touch—glue the peas or lentils to the nose to become the witch's warts.

TRIM 2 EGG SECTIONS AND THE PEAK BETWEEN THEM

DON'T FORGET TO GLUE ON A FEW LENTIL "WARTS"

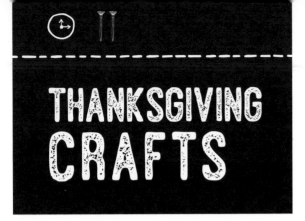

THANKSGIVING CRAFTS

PILGRIM & NATIVE AMERICAN VILLAGE

Building a pilgrim and Native American village is a nice way to get ready for Thanksgiving. For the base, you can use a tabletop covered with butcher paper, or tape down newspapers and paint them with tempera paint. If you use large pieces of cardboard for the base, you can glue the houses and trees in place, and the whole village will be movable.

Remove the staple from the top of the milk carton. Trim with scissors as shown in the drawing. Cut down from the top to 1 inch below the folded edge of the carton at all 4 corners. On the sides with creases, trim off the corners diagonally, leaving a triangle flap on 2 sides. Fold the sides in and restaple at the roofline.

MATERIALS

CARDBOARD

MILK CARTONS (THE SMALL HALF-PINT SIZE SERVED IN SCHOOLS OR ANY SMALL BOXES)

SCISSORS

STAPLER

LIQUID DISH DETERGENT

TEMPERA PAINT

WHITE GLUE

CONSTRUCTION PAPER

YOGURT CONTAINERS (THE SHORT, SQUAT ONES)

GRASS OR HAY

DRINKING STRAWS

MODELING CLAY

GREEN SPONGE

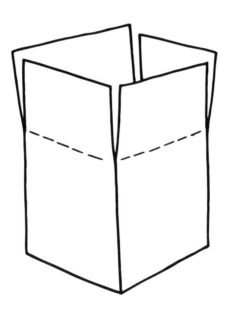

CUT CORNERS
DOWN TO FOLD

CUT AWAY
SHADED AREA

STAPLE ROOF TOGETHER

Add a squirt of detergent to the tempera paint so the paint will adhere to the waxy surface of the cartons. Paint the cabins as desired. When they are dry, glue on paper doors, windows, and details cut from construction paper or draw on with markers.

To make wigwams for the Native Americans, turn the yogurt containers upside down and paint with tempera. When dry, spread with white glue and stick on pieces of dry grass and straw.

To make trees, cut two identical tree shapes from green construction paper. Cut a drinking straw in half, so it's about 4 inches long. Glue the straw between the tree shapes to serve as a trunk. Roll a ball of modeling clay and push the end of the straw into it to stand the tree up.

To make bushes, tear green sponges into pieces and dab with splotches of tempera paint.

PAINT DETAILS ON CABIN

MAKE WIGWAMS FROM
YOGURT CONTAINERS

GLUE A STRAW BETWEEN
2 TREE SHAPES AND STICK THE
STRAW IN MODELING CLAY

DIPPED CANDLES

Fill the saucepan with about 2 inches water and heat it over low heat on the stove. Put the paraffin block into the can then place the can in the water. The paraffin will melt slowly. Add another block of paraffin if you are making a very big candle.

When the wax is melted, lower the wick down into the liquid wax. Then slowly lift it out and hold it until the wax begins to cool and get solid. Then lower the wick again so more wax will coat it. Lift it up and let it cool a little. Repeat this process, over and over, until the candle is the size you want. Then hang it by the wick end to cool. Trim the extra wick off when it is cooled.

MATERIALS

SAUCEPAN

WATER

PARAFFIN

EMPTY CAN

ABOUT 24 INCHES OF CANDLE WICK

CREATE YOUR OWN HOMEMADE DIPPED CANDLES TO USE AT THE FAMILY'S THANKSGIVING TABLE.

WARNING: *ASK AN ADULT TO HELP YOU WITH THIS PROJECT. PARAFFIN WAX CATCHES FIRE EASILY IF IT GETS TOO HOT. DRIPS OF HOT WAX CAN CAUSE BURNS ON YOUR SKIN.*

SNOW-FLAKES

You can make snowflake decorations with toothpicks and miniature marshmallows. Insert toothpicks into marshmallows and connect to other toothpicks.

When you think of winter, you probably think of snow! You can make decorative snowflakes out of lots of things. Folded and cut paper snowflakes are as easy or as complicated as you want to make them. Just fold a piece of white paper several times. Then make a variety of cutouts along the folds. Open up the piece of paper, and it's a snowflake. Just like in nature, no two are the same.

If you want to decorate your windows with painted snowflakes, do it the same way the window painters do for the holidays. Mix white tempera paint with a squirt of liquid dish detergent to make it easier to wash off the windows later. Use a paintbrush and a corner of a sponge to dab on the white paint.

MATERIALS

PAPER

SCISSORS

WHITE TEMPERA PAINT

DISH DETERGENT

TOOTHPICKS

MINI MARSHMALLOWS

FOLD AND CUT SNOWFLAKES FROM PAPER

BUILD SNOWFLAKES WITH TOOTHPICKS AND MINI MARSHMALLOWS

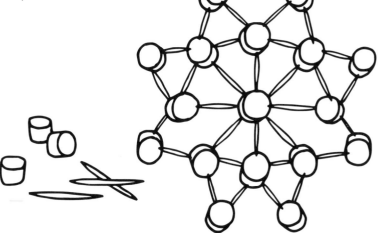

SNOW GLOBE PAPERWEIGHT

Make one of those fascinating old-fashioned snowstorms in a jar for yourself or to give as a gift.

Put something interesting in the jar. You may want to use a small toy such as a tiny snowman or a tiny artificial pine cone and greenery. Use a hot glue gun to secure it to the bottom of the jar if you like. Fill the jar up to 1/4 inch from the rim with water. Spoon in some moth flakes. Put epoxy cement around the rim of the jar and on the jar lid. Screw the jar lid on firmly and let dry completely. When the cement is dry, turn the jar upside down and watch it snow!

SHAKE UP A
SNOWSTORM IN A JAR

MATERIALS

SMALL JAR WITH LID
(A BABY FOOD JAR IS PERFECT)

TINY TOY OR GREENERY

HOT GLUE GUN AND GLUE

WATER

MOTH FLAKES OR GLITTER

EPOXY CEMENT

YARN WREATH

Ask an adult to cut the center part out of the plastic lid with a craft knife, leaving a donut shape about 2 inches thick.

Wrap the green yarn around the lid, securing the ends to the back with glue or tape. As the lid is covered, string on a pony bead here and there to look like holly berries. Cover the whole lid with yarn. Then glue the yarn end to the lid, hiding it under the yarn wrapping.

Tie the ribbon into a bow and glue on at the top of the wreath.

Tie on a piece of fishing line, creating a loop for hanging from the Christmas tree.

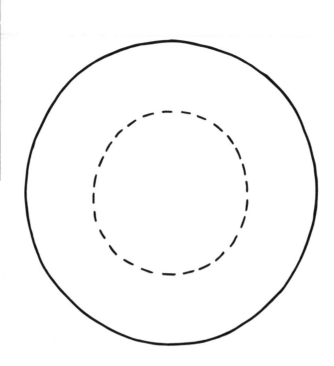

CUT THE CENTER OUT
OF A PLASTIC LID

WRAP WITH YARN, ADD RED
BEADS AS YOU WRAP, AND FINISH
WITH A RED BOW

MATERIALS

COFFEE CAN LID

CRAFT KNIFE

GREEN YARN IN 18-INCH LENGTHS

GLUE & TAPE

12 RED PONY BEADS

1 (24-INCH) PIECE OF RIBBON

FISHING LINE

ANIMAL CRACKER PINS

Make a fun and useful gift for someone you know. Paint an animal cracker cookie with clear acrylic finish or clear nail polish. When it's dry, paint the other side. Then glue it to a jewelry pin back or a magnet.

PAINT WITH CLEAR
NAIL POLISH

GLUE PIN TO BACK
OF ANIMAL COOKIE

MATERIALS

ANIMAL CRACKER

ACRYLIC FINISH OR CLEAR NAIL POLISH

GLUE OR HOT GLUE GUN

JEWELRY PIN BACK

HOLIDAY GIFTS

POTPOURRI

Air-dry the flower petals and leaves. This will take a few days. Use plenty of petals with a proportion of 1 cup petals to 1 tablespoon herbs. In a large container, using your hands, gently mix the flowers, herbs of choice, and orange peel, and cloves if you want. Add the oil, a drop at a time, mixing well after each addition. Store the potpourri sealed in jars. You may want to make a clay or papier-mâché dish to hold your potpourri when you have it out to scent a room. Add another drop of oil to the potpourri when it begins to lose its lovely scent.

MATERIALS

ROSE PETALS (OR ANY OTHER FRAGRANT FLOWER OR LEAVES)

HERBS (LEMON VERBENA, MARJORAM, ROSEMARY)

LARGE CONTAINER

CRUSHED DRIED ORANGE PEEL

CLOVES

ROSE OIL OR LAVENDER OIL

JARS

135

REINDEER

Cut a 6-inch-diameter circle from light brown paper. (Trace around a shortening can lid if you want.) Cut a 6-inch triangle from red paper. Cut antlers for the reindeer by spreading your hand out on the dark brown paper and tracing around it. Trace both hands. Cut out the tracings. Glue the triangle to the circle. Glue the horns so they stick out from behind the head.

Draw on the eyes and mouth with the marker. Use a hole punch to cut dots from the white paper. Glue the dots to the hat to decorate it. Glue the cotton balls to the hat.

Glue 1 red pompom in place for the nose.

MATERIALS

SCISSORS

PENCIL

CONSTRUCTION PAPER: WHITE, LIGHT BROWN, DARK BROWN & RED

GLUE

BLACK MARKER

HOLE PUNCH

COTTON BALLS

RED POMPOM

HANUKKAH MENORAH

Make a menorah to celebrate Hanukkah, the Jewish Festival of Lights. During Hanukkah, Jewish children light a candle every day for 8 days. The candles are placed in a special holder called a menorah. Your menorah can be made in any shape you like. It must hold 9 candles for each day of the holiday, and 1 for the candle used for lighting the other candles, called a shammes or leader.

Shape the clay as you like, flattening the base so it will stand solidly. Insert the candles (birthday candles or special Hanukkah candles) into the clay, pressing an opening a bit larger than the candle. Clays shrink as they dry so be sure to leave space or the candles won't fit. When dry, either bake or fire, depending upon your clay type. Then paint or glaze to finish.

Every night of Hanukkah, add a candle to the menorah.

MATERIALS

CLAY OF YOUR CHOICE

(SEE PAGE 31: REMEMBER CERAMIC CLAYS MUST BE FIRED)

9 SMALL CANDLES

PAINT OR GLAZE

MAKE YOURS IN ANY SHAPE AS LONG AS THERE ARE
8 CANDLES AND ONE TO LIGHT THE OTHER CANDLES

PAPER CHRISTMAS BALLS

Trace 20 (2-inch) circles around a jar lid or similar round item, and cut out the circles.

Fold each circle into a triangle by folding the edges toward the middle in 3 places.

Make the ball by gluing 10 circles together at the folded edges, forming a strip to make the middle of the ball. Glue each end of the strip together to make a circle. Add circles to the center band, creating the top and bottom of the ball. As you glue, hold the edges together or clip with paper clips until dry to keep the ball from coming apart.

When the ball is finished and dry, glue a loop of yarn or ribbon at the top for hanging.

MATERIALS

PENCIL

HEAVY PAPER (OLD CHRISTMAS CARDS ARE GREAT FOR THIS)

SCISSORS

WHITE GLUE

YARN OR RIBBON, ABOUT 6 INCHES LONG

CHRISTMAS TREE TRINKETS

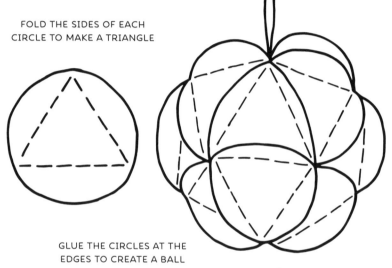

FOLD THE SIDES OF EACH CIRCLE TO MAKE A TRIANGLE

GLUE THE CIRCLES AT THE EDGES TO CREATE A BALL

WINTER BELLS

Cut the carton sections apart and trim away the rough edges. Wrap the carton pieces with aluminum foil, keeping the shiny side out. Smooth it firmly all over. With the point of the scissors, or a sharp pencil point, poke a hole in the top of the bell. Cut a piece of yarn about 4 inches long. Insert one end of the yarn down into the bell. Knot that end. Wrap the knot in aluminum foil, crushing it into a ball shape. You can make several bells and tie them in bunches, or tie single bells to tree branches with the yarn end.

MATERIALS

SCISSORS

EGG CARTON

ALUMINUM FOIL

YARN

STAR OF DAVID PICTURE FRAME

Glue the Popsicle sticks into position to make two separate triangles as shown. Paint or decorate the triangles using markers. Lay 1 triangle on top of the other to form a star. Glue together. Trim your photograph to fit the inside of the star and glue in place. If you want to hang the star, attach yarn or a ribbon at the top.

This is an easy and treasured holiday gift that even the youngest hands can make.

MATERIALS

6 POPSICLE STICKS

PAINT OR MARKERS

GLUE OR GLUE GUN

SCISSORS

PHOTO

YARN OR RIBBON

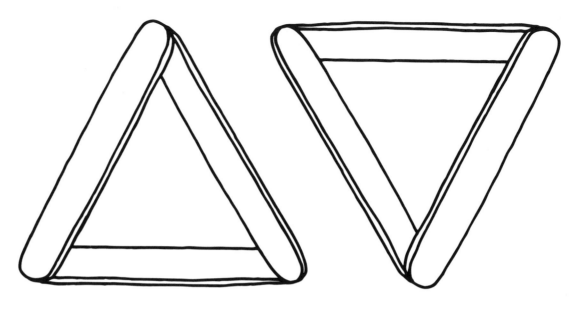

GLUE STICKS TO MAKE
2 TRIANGLES

GLUE ONE TRIANGLE ON TOP OF THE OTHER,
AND GLUE A PHOTO IN THE CENTER

CAROLERS

Begin by making the caroler's body. Fold each page of the magazine down as shown in the diagram. Continue folding until the whole magazine is folded. Sit the body up on old newspapers and spray with red spray paint. Give it a couple of coats so it is completely covered. Even out the pages before you spray so the body looks the same all around.

To form the caroler's head, see the section on papier-mâché, making enough to completely cover a small wad of newspaper. Let the head dry completely. Paint the head a skin tone. Glue the papier-mâché head to the top of the body. A glue gun works very well for this.

Cut out eyes, mouth, and mittens from the construction paper. Glue the face features in place on the head.

Cut out a music book from colored paper. Glue the mitten shapes in place on the book. Glue the book and mittens in place on the front of the body.

Cut the cuff off an old sock. Fold the raw edges to the inside and turn the cuff edge back to create a stocking cap. Glue it in place on the caroler's head.

Use the rest of the sock to cut a long strip to wrap around the caroler's neck for a scarf.

MATERIALS

THICK MAGAZINE, LIKE A READER'S DIGEST

RED SPRAY PAINT

PAPIER-MÂCHÉ FOR CAROLER'S HEAD (SEE PAGE 70)

NEWSPAPER FOR HEAD MOLD

TEMPERA PAINT

HOT GLUE GUN

SMALL PIECES OF COLORED CONSTRUCTION PAPER: RED, BLACK, WHITE

OLD SOCK

FOLD THE PAGE CORNERS TO THE MIDDLE

WALL BANNER

Cut 1 felt square into 2 pieces, 6 x 12 inches each. Lay an 18-inch-long piece of yarn along 1 of the 6-inch edges, placing it 1/2 inch from the cut edge of the felt. Squirt a line of glue along the edge of the felt and fold it back to cover the yarn. Press in place. Let dry.

With scissors, trim off the corners of the bottom of the banner so it comes to a point.

Cut out shapes from other felt pieces and glue them in a decorative pattern. Tie the yarn in a bow at the top and hang on the wall. Add decorations of your choice.

6 INCHES

12 INCHES

TRIM OFF CORNERS

DECORATE BANNER

MATERIALS

SCISSORS

12 X 12–INCH PIECES COLORED FELT

YARN

WHITE GLUE

SEQUINS, BUTTONS, DECORATIVE TRIM

HANSEL & GRETEL'S CANDY HOUSE

Prepare the frosting ahead of time and keep it covered in the refrigerator (it will keep for up to 5 days).

To begin, dab a tablespoonful of frosting on the bottom of the milk carton and stick it firmly in place in the middle of the paper plate. The icing acts as a glue and keeps the house from sliding around on the plate. Then dab a tablespoonful or so of frosting on the back of 4 square crackers. Press them in place against the 4 sides of the carton.

The roof is the tricky part: Dab about 2 tablespoonfuls of frosting on the backs of 2 square crackers. Gently position the crackers on top of the carton, holding them in place to create the roof. It works best if you hold them in place for a minute or so until

the frosting dries a little. Also, if your frosting is too thin, the roof pieces may slide down. Add more confectioners' sugar to stiffen the frosting.

To cover the eaves at the front and back of the house, a small rectangle of cracker can be broken into a triangular shape and attached with frosting. To make it easier for young children, an adult can cover this eave area with frosting, hiding the carton there completely.

Now the house is ready to decorate! Place candy, cereal, or marshmallows onto the frosting before it dries. Spread the roof with frosting and place marshmallows or cereal pieces onto it in rows. Sprinkle confectioners' sugar over the roof to look like a skiff of snow is on the roof. Icicles of frosting can be draped down from the roofline with a spoon. Candies and cereals can be used to create a path, door, chimney, and windows.

To create a beautiful tree, turn a sugar cone upside down and cover it with green frosting. Stick seeds, beans, peas, cereals, or little candies all over it.

Little graham cracker bears or gummy bears might stand in front of the house. Dab some frosting on their bases to securely glue them in place.

These little houses make yummy treats. If you want to save yours, wrap very tightly.

MATERIALS

FROSTING (SEE NEXT PAGE)

MILK CARTONS, 1/2 PINT SIZE, WASHED AND DRIED

STURDY PAPER PLATE FOR EACH HOUSE

GRAHAM CRACKERS, SIX SQUARES FOR EACH HOUSE

ASSORTED SMALL CANDIES FOR DECORATING THE HOUSE

MULTICOLORED MINIATURE MARSHMALLOWS

DRY CEREAL IN ASSORTED SHAPES

ICE CREAM CONE, THE PYRAMID-SHAPED SUGAR CONE TYPE

SEEDS, BEANS, & PEAS

FROSTING RECIPE

1 POUND CONFECTIONERS' SUGAR

3 EGG WHITES AT ROOM TEMPERATURE

1/2 TEASPOON CREAM OF TARTAR

Mix all ingredients in a large bowl with an electric mixer at low speed. Increase the speed to high and beat for about 7 minutes, until the frosting stands in stiff peaks when a knife is pulled through it. This makes about 2 cups of frosting. When making the houses, you will need about 1 cup for each house. Keep this frosting covered at all times, as it dries out quickly. Once dry, it is very hard and keeps the houses and decorations put together for years, if you want to save them.

CANDLE DECORATION

Cover the tissue tube with white paper. Glue. Cut out 2 flame shapes from the yellow paper. Glue them to an open end of the tube, facing each other. Cut out 9 holly leaf shapes from the green paper and 9 red berries from the red paper. Glue the base of each leaf to the bottom of the candle, overlapping leaves slightly as you go around. Glue a red berry to the base of each leaf.

MATERIALS

TOILET TISSUE TUBE

CONSTRUCTION PAPER: WHITE, YELLOW, GREEN, RED

WHITE GLUE

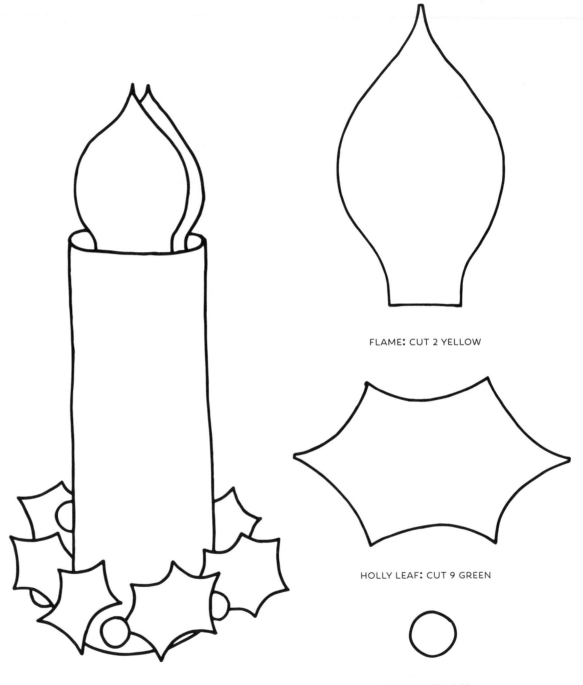

FLAME: CUT 2 YELLOW

HOLLY LEAF: CUT 9 GREEN

BERRY: CUT 9 RED

PUNCHED TIN

Place the cardboard on the tabletop to protect the surface as you hammer on the aluminum.

Draw a design on the paper with a marker. Tape the paper to the pie plate. Use the nail to punch out the design, lightly tapping with the hammer.

To hang, use a glue gun to attach a soda can pop-top ring to the back of the plate.

If you want to make your hanging even fancier, glue lace trim around the edge. Tie a fabric bow and glue it on, too.

MATERIALS

HEAVY CARDBOARD	NAIL AND HAMMER
MARKER	GLUE GUN
PAPER	SODA POP–TOP RING
TAPE	
ALUMINUM PIE PLATES	

MESSAGE SPINNER

Make a spinner that reveals a message as it unwinds. You write half of your message on 1 side and the other half on the back; as it spins, the message blends together right before your eyes!

Cut a circle about 3 inches in diameter from the tagboard. Use a jar lid or a drinking glass for a template if you wish. Punch 2 holes as shown.

Write the first half of your message on one side of the circle. Write the other half on the back of the circle, upside down. Loop the rubber bands through the holes and pull to secure.

To spin the message, slip your index fingers through the rubber bands and wind tightly. Spread your hands apart to let your message spin into view.

MATERIALS

SCISSORS

LIGHTWEIGHT CARDBOARD
OR TAGBOARD ABOUT 5 X 5 INCHES

HOLE PUNCH

MARKERS

2 RUBBER BANDS

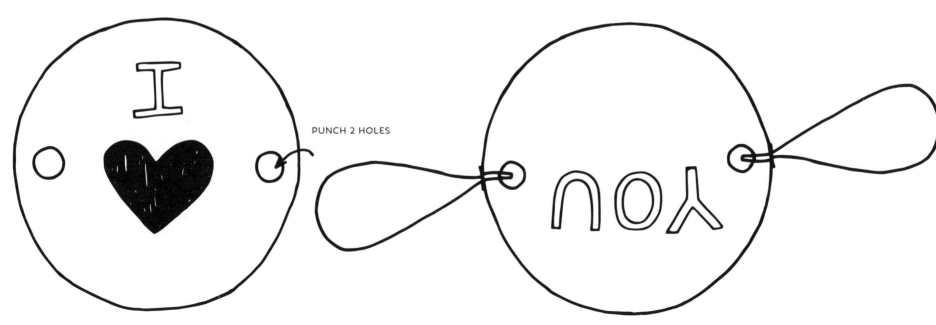

PUNCH 2 HOLES

APPENDIX A

STAGES IN CHILDREN'S ART

Children are ready to try new craft techniques and projects at various stages, just as they are ready for learning to read or write at a particular time in their own development. And, as with academic skills, children first need exposure to and experimentation with the materials before they are ready to turn out finished products.

Most 4-year-olds aren't ready for projects that require long periods of time or precise cutting. Knowing what to expect from children in each developmental stage often helps determine which projects they want to do, as well as which projects they are apt to feel proud of and successful about accomplishing.

Today most educators follow the child development philosophy of psychologist Jean Piaget, who proposed that there are various stages, or levels, through which children advance as they mature and develop more sophisticated thinking and motor skills. The following levels and suggestions for doing art and crafts with children are loosely fashioned after his stages. The ages are merely general time frames; every child develops at the pace most comfortable for him or her.

THE PREOPERATIONAL STAGE: ABOUT 4-TO 7-YEARS-OLD

Children at this level have difficulty observing more than one object at a time. Typically, when pasting or drawing, they are likely to paste or draw one object next to another, rather than overlapping.

When working with these children, use language as you work to help them understand what is going on. Name each object, tool, or material you are working with and talk about what you are doing. Children at this stage want to manipulate materials: finger paint, clay, or anything that is "hands-on" is a favorite for them. They usually can make an outline, and then fill it in. They are quite capable of drawing a picture and coloring it in. They don't need coloring books, which are apt to stifle creativity and spontaneity.

Colors, shapes, and patterns capture their interest, and most children don't relate colors to the natural world. Trees may have a red trunk and blue leaves, which is just fine. Offer lots of bright colors in materials, but not just primary colors as children are fascinated with the wide range that exists. Just sit with a child and a crayon box with many different shades. Children usually want to use them all and want to know what each is named. Rather than limiting the child's palette, always add some interesting pastels or unusual color mixes, like turquoise or magenta, pronouncing the name as you introduce new colors.

Short attention span and limited motor control at this age mean that the sessions and projects are best when quick and easy. Children at any age have trouble sitting around waiting for something to happen, so have supplies and work space ready to go. Many children work on something for about 15 minutes and then grow bored and restless, or they begin to overwork the project and become dissatisfied with it. Cutting accurately with scissors and tracing around a shape may prove difficult with their limited motor skills. They do, however, need to practice those skills. Give them ample time, provide extra materials so they can start over if they want to, and help before anyone becomes frustrated.

Keep supplies of tape, staples, and glue handy. Most children do a lot of patching together as frequently portions of a project are accidentally cut away or parts fall off. Don't guard these supplies or comment on amounts used. Keep them available for the children to use as they need them. If you want to prevent waste, show how to operate the tape dispenser and how to pull the tape across the cutting edge. It is surprising how many young children have never been given a chance to cut a piece of tape for themselves!

Children in the 4-to-7 age group can work individually or in large or small groups, depending upon what is being done. They learn by watching others. When preparing projects for them, keep in mind that an example helps them see what they are attempting to do with the materials they are given. Better yet, prepare several completely different samples, suggesting that there is no one way to do this. The samples should be put away as materials are handed out, before they begin their work. Kids are skillful at copying and want to please adults, so their first response is to recreate your work rather than use their own ideas and interpretations. Encourage expression of their own ideas. Discuss various possibilities and praise all their efforts. Try to have them envision what they think they want to make, and then encourage flexibility along the way. Conversation helps the children express their own ideas. Decision-making (to get started) and thinking about possibilities start the creative thinking process. It is this process which children need to practice, rather than specific practice at "artistic" skills.

During this phase, children are at their most creative. They are usually pleased with their finished projects and don't really seem to care about what their peers think. Adults

working with these children will enjoy the variety and excitement the children bring to their crafts projects.

THE CONCRETE OPERATIONS STAGE: ABOUT 7- TO 11-YEARS-OLD

Children at the Concrete Operations stage are capable of showing perspective and dimension in their drawings. They want to draw, paint, or model in an imitative way. When given an object to duplicate from reality, such as painting a goldfish while sitting in front of a fish bowl, they draw what they know, rather than what they see before them.

In about the fourth grade, children's creativity may begin to slump. They seem to be concerned with realism in depicting things, as well as in the use of color. Children begin to look at spatial concepts. They can draw an object from various angles and show dimension. They understand and use techniques of overlapping.

Fine motor skills are well-developed and children are able to do finely detailed work, manipulating a variety of materials in weaving and sculpture.

In about the sixth grade, children's creativity drops further. They spend their time drawing pictures of the same things over and over, striving for more realism. Their lines tend to be sharp and angular. To counteract this, supply them with a variety of media and techniques. Begin to use an abstract approach to art and craft with them, rather than the stifling realism they tend to fall into. Show them that art is relevant to life; create unique sets of playing cards, dice, decorative paint, and design themes for cars, industrial design, or fashion design. Help them branch out by stretching the limits of what they know.

These preteens are very peer oriented. Those who can reproduce popular cartoon characters or other commercial designs receive recognition from their peers; those who are innovative are not similarly rewarded. As a group, preteens are trying to identify with each other and the larger group in general. Adults are frustrated when working with this age group because these children often refuse to try anything different. In their quest for positive self- esteem, they lose the confidence to think creatively and imaginatively. If they decide they just want to depict the California Raisins accurately, provide the materials and instruction for them to be able to do that. Keep creative thinking alive by discussing other ideas. When ready, they will have the courage to experiment a little.

At all ages, children's work with three-dimensional media, such as clay, mirrors their work with two-dimensional art forms, such as drawing. Thus, children in the first grade who draw people with legs sticking out of a big head will also portray people in that manner using clay. As they begin to incorporate details into their work in one medium, they will do the same in all mediums they are introduced to.

PROCESS VS. PRODUCT: CREATIVE EXPRESSION VS. RESULTS

When working with children and art, one must face a perhaps unspoken dilemma: our own ego and reputation become entwined with the child's finished product. What will others say about our skill, if the finished product is messy, distorted, or simply not "cute"? Frankly, for many adults, it takes a lot of self-control and a good amount of self-confidence to simply let children do their own thing. If you are tempted to do all the cutting and pasting for

the child so it turns out "right," stop and ask yourself: What message am I communicating to this child at this moment?

Try to avoid using precut or precopied cut-and-paste projects with children. These allow for little variation in finished products. The children's finished products may appear "cute" to some adults, and they definitely save time, money (wasted supplies), and adult nerves, but they seriously fail the children. The real catalyst in a successfully creative crafts session for children is an adult who presents the materials, demonstrates some techniques, helps begin to generate some ideas, and then lets the kids go with it.

Encourage the freedom to deviate from the rest of the group by coming up with their own interpretations. Let them learn from their own experimentation and that of those working around them. If Megan tried mixing all the colors together, and the result was mud, she may need to try again to achieve what she had in mind. Meanwhile, those working around her learned a little from watching her trials, and when they try using color in their own ways, they may or may not choose to duplicate her efforts. Again, allow enough time and extra materials for children who decide to start over on their projects. Adults often have false starts and work on refinements along the way in many types of endeavors. Children should have the same freedoms as well.

At all times, the process of creation is more important than the end product. Children learn techniques, skills, and attitudes along the way. Most importantly, they make choices for themselves, developing individuality and self-esteem.

APPENDIX B

WORKING WITH GROUPS OF CHILDREN

When it comes to art and craft projects, kids seem to quickly multiply; if you start with one child, very soon there is a whole group of interested children anxiously waiting to get into the act. These days, with preschool play groups, parents helping other parents by tending their children, and the need for volunteers to run scout troops and to help out in preschools and elementary schools, all of these adults— parents, care-givers, and teachers alike—can benefit from tips on working with larger groups.

There are fewer jobs more demanding or more rewarding than working with children, as anyone who does so regularly can confirm! There must be a special place in heaven, however, for those who face the challenge of working with children during an arts and crafts session! You need the stamina, speed, and footwork of an NFL player, as well as the quick reflexes, eyesight, and steadiness

of nerve of a gymnast. Adults may crumble and dissolve into tears, faced with those chubby hands reaching for the tempera paint all at once. Others have hidden in the closet rather than face helping wild 10-year-old boys during a papier-mâché session. But if you are interested in both children and making things—enough to be using this book—then you must be made of the right stuff!

Attitude is the main tool you need before embarking on a creative project with children. Realize that spills happen, arguments occur, things drip and fall apart, and no one ever cleans up well enough afterward. Once you see the excitement and pride on a child's face when a creation is completed, however, you'll be glad you were a part of it.

CLEANUP

Let's get right to the problem area first. Cleanup. It must be done. Someone must do it. Children are much like adults in this area. Visit an adult art class to see the similarities. Just ask any college-level art/craft instructor what the floor and sink look like after class. (I am convinced that these instructors don't have time to achieve great recognition for their own creative work, because they spend so much time cleaning up after the adults they have in class.) At least the people you and I work with have an excuse. They can't quite reach the sink!

Cleaning up has little appeal for any age group. Children can't seem to see that anything needs cleaning up and adults are either "late for an appointment" or "too tired." When I taught home economics, I was always rewashing the dishes in the classroom kitchen. As an art teacher, I find I am the only one who sees the paint on the floor or that the sink is stopped up. I don't say this to excuse children from participating in cleaning up after a session, only to remind you that they are simply younger and modeling after the adults around them.

Don't feel guilty about offering motivators to children. Offering a reward or prize for getting the cleanup job done usually works wonders. Create contests between several children or groups. Offer a prize for the cleanest work space. This makes everyone responsible, rather than the one obedient child. It gives children a chance to work together, with their friends, sharing a common task.

Setting a time limit helps speed things up. I use a kitchen timer, letting the kids know when I start it.

LIMITING TIME ON TASK

Time limits and creativity don't seem to mix, yet we do live in a very practical world. Children who work slowly sometimes are not finished with a project when the session must end. To help in this area, announce when there are five minutes remaining before cleanup. (Even children who aren't finished must clean up with the others.) If possible, allow the child to continue working on the project at another

time, placing the necessary supplies in a little box. No one likes to get in the way of creativity. Try to work as much as is practical around time constraints.

PLANNING

Planning is an important part of every successful endeavor. Assess the ages, developmental levels, interests, and likes of the children you are working with. Cost and availability of materials are also factors in deciding what to do. Ask yourself what your goal is: to experiment with new media, to try a new technique, to practice a learned skill, or to create a finished item? Weigh all this against time available and attention span of your young craftspeople.

What about the finished project? Kids love to have their work displayed and not just on the refrigerator. Where might it be hung? Will it be given as a gift? If so, is a time limit necessary for completion? Will wrapping paper and card be needed? Will it be exhibited? How will it be labeled, hung, or displayed? What overall theme is being expressed? Will it be sent home with a child when finished? Will it need drying time? Will it need to be wrapped to prevent breakage on the way home? Be sure to let the children

know what will be done with their finished work.

Part of planning the overall project involves setting up the workspace. For some things, children work well individually at desks or in small areas. Sometimes it is easier to put them in small groups or one large group. Six or seven children working at one time is about maximum. If you have more to tend to, give the others something else to do. Then when the group working on crafts is finished, switch. Be sure to give the "waiting group" something else that each can do alone without adult direction.

Keeping the paint and clutter in one area means that all cleanup work is kept to one area as well. And, as we all work with limited supply budgets, dividing large groups into smaller ones means that you only have to obtain brushes or tools for the seven or ten children who are working on a project at one time. This way all your supply money isn't put into only one or two media. I made the mistake of ordering twenty-four watercolor sets my first year of teaching. Rather than tie up money in so many sets, I could have ordered twelve watercolor sets and twelve sets of pastels. Or, better yet, six sets each of pastels, colored pencils, markers, and other media. Then, at each art session, the children could rotate through the various media, all working on a common theme in a variety of media.

If you receive donations of some items but not enough for everyone, rotate the children so they can have a variety of experiences. It sometimes makes it more interesting when each group is working with something different and all can observe and discuss the different results.

Logistically, if you plan for the group rotating in four separate media, you can save yourself planning work because you can use that same plan for four art sessions, before each child has used all the media. This obviously works better with older children. Before attempting anything like this with little ones, be sure you have some additional adult assistance.

When working at long tables, using a messy medium such as tempera or papier-mâché, I like to remove the chairs. The children seem to spill less when they are already standing up, the chairs stay a lot cleaner, and more kids can fit at a table. Children don't seem to tire during art (because they are busy and engrossed in having fun!) and the chairs aren't missed. As a matter of fact, many children work better when they can wiggle around or simply shift from one foot to another.

Tables can be covered with newspaper, large sheets of butcher paper taped down, or draped with old vinyl shower curtains. I favor the shower curtain because it stays flat and can be set up quickly. When finished, roll it up, take it home, and wash in the washer. I have also cut shower curtains into desk-size pieces, useful when children are working at a desk or small area. They can get their own shower mats, cover their desks, and later roll or fold them up and put them away. These can also be washed with a sponge or in a washer.

Part of the preplanning necessary for a successful art session includes getting supplies ready. Avoid putting out stacks of colored paper, bottles of glue, and whatever else in bulk. Children crowd and argue over what to take and how much to use. If you want your whole session to go smoothly, supplies should be arranged ahead of time.

Prepour the glue or paste into smaller containers or assign a child to begin doing this before it's needed. Cut paper to the size needed or into sizes that are manageable for the children's ages. Precut drinking straws, have pipe cleaners divided up, and sort small items. Assemble small items on paper plates for each child to take to the work area.

Arrange everything so that each child can come up, take what is needed, and leave the supply table immediately. If things are handed out individually, distribute them before the children arrive. After the children are settled, let them know that there are ample extra supplies for them to come up and get when needed. While this preplanning is not meant to narrow the children's experiences, it is a vital part of group management in order to ensure that the children are able to participate equally without frustration due to lack of supplies when needed.

Have completed samples for the children to see and touch. Display some models where they can all see. If possible, have photographs of inspirational ideas for them to absorb. Preplanning time and discussion results in more creativity and exploring the potential of materials.

While you display and talk about some possibilities, the kids are tossing these stimuli around in their heads, and their project is already beginning to take shape. They begin making decisions based on what they like and don't like, what they might like to try, and what piques their interest. Some children start immediately while others need to toss around ideas more, and still others lack the confidence to start at all. When this happens, help them begin so the experience is a positive one.

Creating the sample project takes time, but as you do it, try to see it through the child's eyes. Smooth out all the rough spots that might develop as they are working on it. Keep your samples to use again later. I like to collect photographs of successful or unusual children's projects and display these before the kids begin. They enjoy seeing what other children have done, and it often frees them up to try some creating themselves.

LABELING PROJECTS

Labeling finished projects is one of those seemingly little details that can take on monster proportions and actually ruin an experience. Children in the primary grades often are not able to identify their finished crafts, creating arguments over whose is whose. Some children help themselves to the finished projects they like best, regardless of whose name is on it. Try to keep finished work displayed away from the door, making sure that children retrieve their own items with adult supervision.

DISPLAYING WORK

How to best display finished projects can sometimes become a challenge. Use cardboard boxes, covered with wallpaper or paint, to create four-sided displays atop a table. Boxes can also be covered or painted, weighted down with a brick inside, to become pedestals for display of three-dimensional work.

If children work on the same size paper most of the time, precut mats work well. Display on the wall with different children's works matted each week. Nothing makes a picture quite as special as a mat or frame and a place on the wall.

Work hung on the walls can sometimes be stapled up, but if

you want to avoid putting small holes in the work, and the wall, use the synthetic substance that remains adhesive and can be used over and over. Sold in the office supply section of many food and drug stores, it can be rolled back into a ball and used many times.

RECYCLING FOR GRAB ART

No one likes to throw away any portion of materials that can be recycled for another project. Keep boxes for scraps of colored paper, yarn, mat board, or anything else that can be used again. Save empty shampoo bottles to store unusual shades of paint. Keep a clean covered trash can in the corner to save items for Grab Art projects.

When you have a supply of assorted bits and pieces of sequins, yarns, fabric scraps, colored tissue papers, wallpaper sample pages, and whatever else, begin to fill Grab Art bags. Use brown paper lunch sacks, filling each one with assorted odds and ends. Fold over the top of each bag and staple once. When you have enough bags for everyone, you are ready for a truly creative make-it session.

Children select bags, go to their seats, and open them. Using only the items found in the bag, each child creates something of his or her choice. Provide tape, glue, paste or staples, and sheets of paper or colored tagboard. Let their imaginations go wild. If some children need prompting at first, suggest a variety of things to do: puppets, bookmarks, sculptures, toys, outer space creatures, mobiles, or whatever else the materials seem to suggest.

Grab Art also helps use up the bits and pieces of supplies that are too good to throw away but are in limited supply. Kids love Grab Art. Maybe it's because of the mystery of what is in their bag, as well as the no-holds-barred approach to creating.

HANDLING GLUE AND PASTE

You probably already buy glue in quantity and pour into smaller dispensers for the children's use. For the small bottles necessary, you can save mustard, ketchup, or shampoo bottles.

You may want to dilute white glue with a little water. Younger children often find white glue too thick to work with; it spreads more easily and dries faster when slightly diluted.

Glue sticks are an all-time favorite because they can be used easily, store easily, and don't make a mess. The only drawback is their expense. Hot glue guns work well with many materials, but adults should operate these.

USING PAINTS WITH KIDS

Tempera is the most common paint found in children's craft programs. It has bright colors, is easy to handle, and is inexpensive. If you add a little liquid dish soap to each container of liquid paint, it cleans up and washes out of clothing more easily. The soap also helps tempera adhere better to glossy surfaces such as glass or plastic. Collect covered containers to store paint in: baby food jars with lids, yogurt containers, and even small milk cartons with a clothespin to pinch the top closed are all useful.

When setting paints out for children's use, I find it much easier to mix up several colors, providing a brush or two for each container. Then, children simply ask for the

color they need and pass it and its brush on to the next one who needs it. This avoids the need for children to rinse out brushes between changes of color while using tempera. The children can focus on applying color, rather than fussing with brushes.

For older children, egg cartons work very well as paint holders. Give them squirts of the basic colors, allowing them to mix additional colors in the remaining cups. This allows them to work independently of others at the table. The egg cartons can be rinsed out and left to drain in the sink for repeated use. When older children paint with acrylic paints, egg cartons can be used to store their palette until the next session. Close the carton and label, then overwrap with freezer wrap and fasten with tape. Then store the cartons in a freezer, and when the children are ready for the next session, the paints will still be moist and usable.

When mixing paint, try to mix a few unusual shades for younger children, too. I always include pink and at least two shades of blue. If white is added to the basic primary colors, the finished works take on a brighter and happier tone, pleasing to most children. Bright, clear pastel shades are always favorites.

Give the children a limited palette. Tell the children that they are free to use any or all of what's available, but that the colors provided are the choices for this session. Pick a variety of colors so each child can express the mood he feels from what is available.

Paper color should be considered carefully before a painting session, too. Use light colored construction paper with dark colors of paint; darker colors of paper help pastel shades show up better. Stunning results can be obtained by painting bright, jewel-toned construction paper with colors lightened with a bit of white paint.

Most paintbrushes have handles that are simply too long for children who are working on tabletops. They are awkward for a child to manipulate and contribute to spills of paint containers. I like to cut the handles off a bit so children can manage them more easily. The longer brush handles are fine for

easel painting, as they enable the child to stand back from the paper while painting.

Collect varied types of brushes. Save cosmetic brushes and applicators, pick up some sponge applicators sold in hardware stores, and use cotton swabs or pieces of torn sponge for applying paint. Dried-out, felt-tipped markers can be used to daub on paint.

Paint shirts or smocks are a necessity. No parent appreciates a ruined outfit, no matter how creative the child. I ask parents to send paint smocks or old shirts, but I also like to provide a selection of discarded men's short sleeve dress shirts, which give maximum coverage with minimum fuss.

Provide a drying area for completed projects. Use masking tape on the floor to delineate a protected area or use clothesline and clothespins to hang completed work out of harm's way.

AVOID DISAPPOINTMENTS

Don't become dismayed when things don't seem to be working out. Juggling children's varied ages, abilities, and interests often makes it difficult to complete projects together. There are some shortcuts for helping those who are falling

behind. Use a portable hair dryer to blow-dry papier-mâché animals and tempera paintings. Sometimes you may have to staple something that really should be glued. You may want to provide some precut or preformed pieces for emergency use. This is by no means a crutch to make sure the project looks "right." Children become disappointed at not completing their work and get discouraged halfway through the session if they realize completion is impossible.

Try to find some way for each child to complete a simpler version of a project, rather than sending them home with a bag of assorted dinosaur body parts and instructing him to attempt putting them together on their own at home. The child with a completed project is a lot happier and leaves with positive feelings about the session, and arts and crafts as well.

MONEY-SAVING SUBSTITUTES

When using charcoal, chalk, or pastels, the work must be sprayed with a fixative to prevent smearing. Rather than purchasing the expensive fixatives sold in art supply stores, I find that the cheaper brands of hairspray work very well. Do the spraying in a well-ventilated area or step outside to spray.

Many craft projects need a shiny gloss coating. You can purchase a wide variety of spray or brush-on coatings. I have found that using the less expensive brands of acrylic floor wax works just as well, is no problem when used in a room without ventilation (because there are no problem vapors), and clean up easily with soap and water. I have used floor wax on ceramics, papier-mâché, dough art, and sawdust clay projects with great success. Pour the wax into containers and provide paintbrushes for the children to coat their own objects. You may want to give the items more than one coat for better protection and a brighter shine.

Another money-saving finisher is shoe polish. It can be rubbed into plaster, hardened clay, and papier-mâché surfaces, and polished with a soft cloth until it has a dull sheen. Give it a shiny coat of wax, too, if desired.

Latex paints offer a viable alternative when you are making large projects, such as a mural or large papier-mâché or cardboard constructions. If you watch for yard sales and collect from friends' and parents' garages, you can come up with a variety of latex paint colors. Mix the paints to achieve the colors you desire. The range will be from deep darks to pastels, rather than bright colors. Latex also makes an excellent base coat for papier-mâché and cardboard constructions, which can then be painted over with watercolors or tempera.

MISCELLANEOUS TIPS

Sometimes it's fun to use easels for children's paintings, but they are costly and difficult to store when not being used. A simple table easel can be made by cutting the sides of a box at an angle and propping a drawing board or larger piece of sturdy cardboard across the opening. Tape or staple the child's paper to the drawing board surface. Children can store drawing supplies inside the box until the next time they're used.

When setting up your supply area and dividing materials out for children, I often find paper plates make good organizers. When making craft items, using inexpensive paper plates gives the children an individual work surface. They can put their name on their plate (especially necessary when doing clay or dough art sculpting). The plate provides a drying and display area, too.

If you run out of glue or paste, a simple substitute can be made for use with paper projects. Mix flour and water until it is gravy- like. The mixture can be used for papier-mâché as well.

Visit your local newspaper printing plant and ask about their newsprint roll ends. They usually have some paper left on the rolls when the newspaper is printed, and they will often give them to you or sell them for a small fee. This paper is thin but useful for covering table tops and for free drawing.

Wallpaper sample books, carpet-end pieces, mosaic tiles, and fabric remnants are all valuable to the arts and crafts program. Storage of these finds is a problem. I like to use empty paper boxes with lids. Ask a printer or copy center for them. The boxes can be labeled and stacked. Also, plastic garbage cans with lids are useful to drop items in until you have time to sort and file away.

When storing lace, trims, or yarn, wrap around empty tissue tubes. It keeps them untangled and it makes it easier to dispense.

One of the most useful items in a craft studio is discarded cardboard trays used to separate stacks of canned goods in the grocery store. They are yours for the asking and can be used to store paper or finished work, as a work area for children at their seats, or to set out supplies in an orderly manner. Because of their price (free) and availability, just toss them out when they get worn.

If you've visited a "hands-on" children's museum recently, you've probably noticed a recycling center where children can buy bags of manufacturers' odds and ends for pennies. You, too, will find local manufacturers very willing to donate barrels of by-products including dowels, foam pieces, felt, plastic shapes, metal pieces, cardboard, and swatches of materials. The variety is amazing and the price is great—free for the asking.

Manufactured in China in January 2021 by Paramount Printing
First Edition
25 24 23 22 21   5 4 3 2 1

Published by
Gibbs Smith
P.O. Box 667
Layton, Utah 84041
1.800.835.4993 orders
www.gibbs-smith.com

Designed by Nicole LaRue

Gibbs Smith books are printed on paper produced from sustainable PEFC-certified forest/controlled wood source. Learn more at www.pefc.org.

Library of Congress Control Number: 2020942332

ISBN: 978-1-4236-5737-8

DISCLAIMER: Some of the activities suggested in this book require adult assistance and supervision. Children and their parents or guardians should always use common sense and good judgment in playing, cooking, and making crafts. The publisher and author assume no responsibility for any damages or injuries incurred while performing any of the activities in this book; neither are they responsible for the results of these recipes or projects.

LAURIE CARLSON

Laurie Carlson, M.Ed. and Ph.D., has written 22 books, including a Washington state history textbook currently used in public schools. She has taught grades K-3, and as an adjunct professor for the history departments at Western Oregon University, Eastern Washington University, and Washington State University-Pullman. She has also taught classes in writing nonfiction at Eastern Washington University, and technical writing at Washington State University-Spokane. She currently lives in Coeur d'Alene, ID.